Take It From A Teenager

Scott Bradbrook

A catalogue record for this work is available from the National Library of Australia

First paperback edition January 2020

Illustrations by Friska Maulani
Cover Design by PixelStudio
Photography by Max Ryszawa

ISBN: 978-0-6487577-8-8 (paperback)
ISBN: 978-0-6487577-0-2 (ebook)

Published by Scott Bradbrook
www.scottbradbrook.com

TO YOU, MY DEAR READER

Although this book began as a dream of a much smaller and less educated 14-year-old me, it is dedicated to you, my esteemed audience. Until now, I never thought that this book would be possible. I never could have done it without you. For keeping me going through the hard times and reminding me why I decided to write this book, I am truly grateful.

CONTENTS

ACKNOWLEDGMENTS

Although a lot of hard work and effort went into the production of this book on my part, there are a few people I have to thank for it. First, I'd like to thank God for blessing me with the skills and knowledge to produce such a book. I know I'm not perfect, but with your blessing and guidance, I will continue to strive to be better.

I would like to thank my parents, Steve and Nelly Bradbrook, who helped me with the editing and growing the idea in the beginning. I can never express the amount of gratitude I have for everything you have done and given up for me. I hope that what I have produced in this book makes you proud.

I would like to thank my two sisters, Melissa and Krystle Bradbrook. Thank you for loving and supporting me. I hope I make both of you proud of me too.

A big thank you belongs my good friend Max Ryszawa for the photography. Thank you for always being there for me and inspiring me to be a better person.

To Friska Maulani, I am deeply grateful for the outstanding illustrations and PixelStudio for the awesome cover. These aspects brought my vision to life. For that I am thankful.

Although I won't be able to name all of you, I'd like to thank my friends and teachers who have been with me along the way in writing this book. Very few of you knew I was even writing one in the first place, but you all played a very significant role in inspiring, motivating, educating and guiding me to what I am today. For that, I am and always will be, eternally grateful.

And last but not least, the largest thanks and acknowledgement belongs to 14-year-old Scott Bradbrook. You had the courage to do something new and different. I hope I make you proud most of all. Thank you.

CHAPTER 1: ME, MYSELF & I

Some stories begin with a misfortunate beginning and end with happily ever after. However, my story is just as ordinary as the next. I was born in South Australia in 2001. My story has only begun as I am only 15 when writing this, and 18 when editing. The only thing is, I seem to have come across knowledge beyond my years. It's quite funny when you think about it, that the oldest aren't always the wisest. However, that is not to say that the smartest are the youngest. What I'm trying to say is that my story has only begun, but I've had quite a learning journey along the way.

This book is written in the perspective of a teenager, but not your typical one. If you think about the average teenager, you will probably think of a boy or girl with their headphones in their ears, on social media or some sort of device in their own little world. You may also think of teens taking selfies and the endless posts just for the likes on Facebook or hearts on Instagram. I have come across many sorts of teens that are different from one another, but not like me. At the same time, I am not perfect. Although I may aspire to reach perfection, it is a goal one can never achieve.

My story is one of many teenagers that are out there. I began my schooling at St Francis of Assisi primary school in Newton, then continued onto Christian Brothers' College Adelaide; a school I have flourished at and am proud of. Raised in a home full of support, love and my two sisters, I grew up to know the difference between right and wrong. My parents are Steve and Nelly Bradbrook. My mum is Filipino, and my dad is Australian. My sisters are both over ten years older than me, making me the baby of the family.

When growing up, I wasn't always the coolest kid in the playground. Often, I was judged for being the nerdy one, the kind one, the one who cared that something or someone was being hurt and I did my best to prevent that. Unfortunately, lessons were learnt the hard way. However, these lessons have made me a stronger person today. Currently, I am still the same young man trying to fit in at school (now university) and find myself.

Being recognised as "the nerd" in my group, I often get criticised for it. Then again, I should be proud of what I am. Another factor within being a nerd is that people aren't afraid to say it to your face. Over the years, I have learnt to take it as a compliment. My beginning is a typical one. One with friends, family and the standard growing up issues.

Music is a unique language that very few truly understand. It can be hard to cope with what life throws at you. Sometimes, even I find it hard to deal with everything. But that is why music is my escape. I can be in my own world of pop, alternate, RnB, indie or any genre I feel like. Some like to listen, others participate, and when we all get together as a whole, we can create something that was never thought possible before. I have met many people through music and am glad to have met those people. It has opened me up and given me the confidence I need to achieve what was once before unachievable.

"Reading is knowledge and knowledge is power."

Although it may not seem like it, reading is a whole other world of its own. Being in the safety of ink and paper, stories come to life as the reader lifts each word off the page. Having that much power to change the world is incredible, which is why most people choose to read or write books. The power behind reading isn't often acknowledged in any book or speech. It is in reading that we learn lessons the easy way and not the hard way. If the world couldn't read, the only way to communicate information would be through word of mouth or pictures. It makes you realise how powerful words are and that:

"The pen is mightier than the sword."

Although this quote is overused, I believe that it isn't the pen itself, but what is written with it that counts.

Now that I think back to the times I read short books just to get a title on the Reading challenge, I regret it. I didn't give enough time to read books that took me on a journey to somewhere else. Over many years now, I have read all kinds of texts, novels and manuals. The ones that mean more to me are known as PMA books (or positive mental attitude books for those who don't know what PMA stands for). Books like "Think and Grow Rich" by Napoleon Hill, "The Secret" by Rhonda Bryne, and "The Seven Habits of Highly Effective People" by Norman Vincent Peale. By reading books like these, I have gained so much insight about the world around me. When reading these books with my dad, I am constantly intrigued by the amount of information they can fit into a single chapter. Some books seem choppy and disorienting, constantly changing subjects without any flow or consistency. However, the PMA books that I have read seem to flow and link each concept to another continuously. This is a big change from the usual novels that I used to read (which I still do occasionally)

Change is inevitable in life. Some people are afraid of it because they enjoy consistency. By gaining a better understanding of what it means to be a teenager in combination with the lessons I have learnt from the power of reading, I have made some changes in my life. This may be with the people I choose to be around or my response to certain situations. None the less, changes have had to be made. I am constantly being bombarded with nagging social trends, peer pressure and the other stresses of being a teenager. Somehow, I have learned to cope with these pressures, as most of them are minor annoyances.

I used to associate with a lot of negative people when I was younger. Little did I know then, I was being corrupted and driven to breaking point. Eventually, I had a realisation when one of my good friends left my group. After making the "courageous decision" to leave myself, my old group of friends soon dispersed and branched off. Now I surround myself with people who I know I can trust and who I feel comfortable around. People who weren't afraid to be different, to be themselves no matter what anyone said or did.

These sorts of people are seen less and less in the ever-changing world around us. As society grabs hold and shakes the 'human' out of people, we are becoming more like robots (or more so broken machines). You see the man in the cubicle next to you, continually worrying about a big job he has to do, only to find out that he has three more days to complete what hasn't been started yet. You see the woman at the shops who is always screaming at her kids to behave. The people you see in the same circumstances are the robots.

We need to choose to be human and take control of ourselves. Too often we forget that we need to pause and think about how other people are feeling, how we are feeling, and then react accordingly. In my years of schooling, I've seen many kids rushing into stupid situations just because they want attention. You see the boy at the front always raising his hand to answer the question (which used to be me in many cases) only to be interrupted by the dumb kid in the back asking what subject they are doing. We need to stop neglecting the feelings of ourselves and others and make sure that we properly connect with people. Not over the internet, but face to face.

CBC is my current high school community. It consists of over 700 students in the senior college and is the place I call home (editor's note: I now call the University of Adelaide my home as of 2019). I am proud to be called a Christian Brother. My school before CBC was called St Francis of Assisi. It was a small school that seemed big at the time. I am also proud to call myself a Bradbrook. My heritage can be traced back to England (specifically Essex). It is quite amazing what my ancestors have done to get the Bradbrook name to what it is today. I admire the fact that my great, great, great grandfather arrived here on a convict boat and came into owning land near my current residence. My great grandfather fought in World War 1 in the 48th battalion. He then returned from the war to have nine children. It amazes me every time I think about how I come from a long line of brave men. But it was their choice to be brave, not something they were born with.

"Choice" is a single syllable word that has the power to change everything. Choosing to hold the right morals and faith guides the decisions we make. Being raised in a strong Christian family, I was taught to know and love God and what Jesus did for the world. It's not something that the typical teenager would talk about considering most teenagers aren't as involved in religion as others are. Having to decide between social trends and God is a big issue that many people face today; whether they should keep the commandments of God or obey the rules of a new trend. This is a strong topic that I will be talking about in a further chapter. I encourage all people to find their faith and to know that God is with them on their journey in life.

Religious, academic and life morals are hard to align, as they all have a small area where they disagree. Being raised to know the difference between right and wrong was a major lesson I learnt from my parents. School taught me about discipline, and that putting the date in the top right-hand corner of your page is worth an extra mark. Religion taught me that it's okay that I'm not perfect, but I should strive to be my best. Having these morals and more has led me to the conclusion that some teenagers neglect or simply don't have any morals. I continuously question other people (mostly in my head) about their morals. Everyone encounters a few people that seem to be reckless and endanger the safety and sanity of themselves and other people around them. You always question yourself, "what were they thinking when they did this", or "why did they do that". To put this to rest, I will be talking about the importance of having the right morals in a further chapter which opened my eyes and the eyes of my previous readers. Knowing that people are different and that their morals can disagree helps with being empathetic and making real connections. But more importantly, having the correct morals supports correct decision making.

Work isn't always the most fun. It's hard to learn how to like work. At the beginning of my learning, academic performance was not at the front of my mind. Back then, I only thought about getting through another lesson without losing focus on what the teacher was saying. However, in recent years, I have upped my game and put more of a focus on how I perform academically. By focusing on the work that I need to achieve, I have generated strategies for effectively completing the work the needs to be done. These strategies are not yet perfected as nothing can ever be perfect. There is always room for improvement.

One of these strategies is surrounding myself with people of my intellect or above. By surrounding myself with people that I want to be like, eventually, I can learn from them and vice versa. This is yet another chapter that will be discussed in the future. Once I began to change who I associated with, I started finding hope and a place where I could be myself without being judged or criticised.

Age is just a number to many people, but what is your number? See, my number is only 15 (when writing this, but 18 when editing) and many people question me and my intellect. At the beginning of this chapter, I mentioned briefly that my story has only begun, which is true. But I have been told more than enough times that I have an old soul. The first time I heard this, I was a little confused. I pictured a small, old man holding up a book that read "stuff I know". I thought to myself, "that was not a nice thing to say", only to realise that it was a metaphor for me having knowledge beyond my years. The reason my story has only begun is that I'm only a teenager. My plan for life isn't crystal clear as I'd like it to be, and I have no idea what to expect. But what I can do for now is use my knowledge to help other people. Knowing that there are people like me is encouraging. I often think about what would happen if someone told me to act the age I know. I'd probably be too old. But for now, I will enjoy being a teen.

Teenagers aren't known for their wisdom in this day and age. They are known for their trends and technology. Like the selfie, the ridiculously short shorts that show EVERYTHING, Facebook, Snapchat, Instagram, and that's only to name a few. Not to brag, but my perspective is quite different from the typical teenagers. I mean, you are reading this book, aren't you? And you've come this far in my perspective, which only proves my point.

Making a difference in this world is a hard thing to do. But it needs to be done, nevertheless. Making every decision count is a core pillar of my perspective and what I aim for in life. Throughout this book, you will see people that have stories similar to mine, and I am proud to know them. These are vital for my generation as I do not wish to be labelled the "selfie generation" or the "me, myself and my iPhone generation". I've written this book to prove the existence of diamonds in the rough of this generation and am hoping you notice them too. By getting the word out, I hope to encourage more young, like-minded individuals to voice out and show what they are capable of as a new generation.

Learning from a teenager may not always be the best thing if you're talking to an average teen. People will criticise me and judge the information I provide in this book. But once you get off your high horse (all you critics out there), you will realise that what I have to say should be taken seriously. It's not only directed to adults but teens as well. It's primarily directed to those who would take on the concepts, understand them, and use them. This book can be used by anyone, of any age, of either gender, of any background.

Using the strategies, skills and tips in this book is entirely up to you. Whether or not the information leaps from the pages is up to you. However, I encourage it strongly. When reading this book, it is also important to acknowledge the skills and examples provided. What I have to say is important. What anyone has to say is important really, and there are people you will meet that say everything but nothing important.

On the other hand, you will also meet people who don't say anything but need to say something important. All people in life deserve to be heard, and that is a common fact. Once you accept the fact that you want to be heard, you also need to accept that you need to listen as well. Sit back and relax. Take it from a teenager.

CHAPTER 2: I'M WAITING

Patience is a virtue. All good things come to those who wait. You've probably heard these sorts of quotes before, but you may be puzzled about the importance of waiting. Many people lose their patience and suffer the drastic consequences for their impatience. Consider the person who cuts you off in traffic, suffers a fatal car accident and is now paralysed. It could have been you, but someone was too impatient to realise it's a 60 zone. Another less extreme example is with cooking. If you take the cake out of the oven too early, it won't taste good because it is under baked. Regardless of the situation, there is no excuse for people to be impatient.

When making moral decisions, it is important to wait and be patient. Too often, people make sudden decisions they later regret. Successful results can only be achieved within a specific time frame. It's not only about being patient; it's about having good timing.

Patience is defined as the ability to stay calm in a problematic or irritating situation. Not many people understand what being patient truly means. Some people may have personal definitions that relate to their current circumstance. The mother with her nagging kids might say, "patience is not screaming at my kids every time they nag me for something". An office employee may say, "patience is waiting for something to happen or while something is happening". Patience is about having the right attitude when you are waiting.

Impatience and patience both have emotional links that allow people to read how you are. Often when people lose their tempers, they are impatient. This can be seen in their reaction to a specific circumstance. Patient people usually stay calm and take the situation in a relaxed manner. The difference between a person who is patient and a person who isn't is their choice.

"In-between stimulus and response, there is a place called choice."

The way you react to a situation is entirely up to you. If someone cuts you off in traffic, (which is the stimulus), you can either choose to:

a) Yell at them even though you know they can't hear you

b) Beep your horn and wave your hands frantically at them

c) Choose to react calmly and humbly

After all, one wrong decision can impact you dramatically. Having unknown emotional links between patience and impatience is quite interesting. When you are impatient, you compromise calm and positive thinking, which is a real issue today considering the amount of negativity in the world.

Surrounding yourself with less irritating situations isn't the easiest thing to do. There will be stress-packed situations in life, guaranteed. When you are patient, you are calm and positive. Listening also connects with patience. When people are speaking to you, you choose to listen to them in a specific way. The four more common types of listening are as follows.

- The first type is block listening. This occurs when we translate any incoming words as "blah, blah, blah". We may also convert them into silence and block any incoming information completely.

- Type two is rebuttal listening. This is when you don't really listen to what the other person is saying and instead prepare something to say back at them. This often occurs in arguments between people and can be very hard to maintain.

- The third type of listening is partial listening, which is where you only hear what you want to.

- The final kind of listening is common listening. This is where you listen to what the other person has to say and fully consider that information.

Several other listening types have branched off from this, such as emotive listening where you consider the other person's perspective. Deciding which way to listen is all a matter of choice.

Decisions aren't always easy to make. I could sooner make a three-course meal than I could decide which movie to stream. Choices are tough to make, and deadlines don't make these decisions any easier. You can't control what is going on around you. But you can control yourself. You can change the way <u>you</u> approach a situation.

Attending a youth conference the other week, I received the opportunity to listen to speakers Peter Toganivalu, David Hall and Micah Berteau. I enjoyed all their speeches, but I was most intrigued by the talks given by Peter Toganivalu. He admitted that he was an emotional wreck, which made me cautious about what I was in for. He went on to speak about how he was highly passionate about changing the name of our generation to something a lot less stereotypical than the "me, myself and my iPhone generation".

"Some people claim to be emotional wrecks without understanding that they are simply passionate."
– Peter Toganivalu

People like Peter Toganivalu and the other speakers all have one thing in common. They are open to speaking to people about their emotions and are willing to help people through whatever they are going through. All speakers truly inspired me, and I recommend that anyone reading should see them if you get the chance.

Life isn't always sunshine and rainbows as many people have come to know the hard way. But being patient can prevent many of the accidents or unfortunate incidents that happen in our lives. Waiting a few more moments here or there could be the turning point in someone's life. Being patient at the right times isn't always easy. But there is hope for everyone. No matter how impatient they may be, there is hope that everyone can have patience. In the times when you are patient, you grow. It reminds me of a famous quote that I can't put word for word, but it goes something like:

"You can't pull up the roots of a plant to see how well it's growing"

This may mean something completely different to what I believe it means, but that's beside the point. I think the quote means that we need to give the situation, people and things time and patience to grow. You can't expect to plant the seed and have a fully-grown plant within 3 to 5 working days. It needs time to grow, which is something many people neglect. People tend to become impatient in tough times because they want to see the results now. We need to learn how to be patient and let it grow.

Stop! Wait a minute. Some of you might get that reference and are rolling your eyes at me. If you didn't, good. But I still have a point here. You need to stop.

Most people go through the day constantly on the move; always going from one place to the next, one agenda to another, one person to the next. Sometimes we need time to stop and breathe. It's like going into a food eating marathon. You can either stop at the end with your whole body filled with burgers and fall into a food coma of regret. Or you can stop, breathe and rethink the situation before you stuff yourself with over 35 burgers.

An old advertisement quite a few years ago showed a woman in an office talking to her assistant about their ad in the Yellow Pages. You see her start to count to ten and the secretary legs it out of the building, only to have the original woman scream "NOT HAPPY JAN!" out the window. That's not really the point I wanted to make. The woman stopped and counted to 10. Doing this helps you clear your mind and think about your response. Sometimes your response is instant, and you can't help that. But we need to try as much as we can to stop, breathe, count to ten (calmly) and handle the situation accordingly (whether it is "NOT HAPPY JAN" or not).

Sentences are powerful. Words are even more powerful. But have you ever considered the power of a comma? Many people underestimate the power of grammar in a piece of text, but it can make all the difference. Over the many years I have been reading PMA books, I have come across many examples of "the power of a pause" as I like to call it. From a book called The Power of Blessing by David Timms, he writes the following example:

"A woman, without her man, is nothing."

This can be compared to the reverse statement with the same words but different grammar:

"A woman; without her, man is nothing."

Now you can finally understand the power of a comma. But that isn't the only thing that I'm talking about. Reading with patience is important. Taking time to read every single word in this book requires patience, and proper reading can only be achieved with patience. The other day, I was reading a post on Facebook.

It had a photo which read:

"what is wrong with the the following sentence…

a, b, c, d, e, f, g, h, i, j, k, l, m, n, o, p, q, r, s, t, u, v,

w, x, y, z".

Initially, I couldn't see it at first. Then I re-read the sentence and noticed something I didn't see before because I was impatient. If you want, you can re-read it and see if you pick up on it. Not many people take the time to read every word. A word can be the difference between life and death, one and one million, even success and failure.

Success can never be achieved without patience. But why does growing take time? The answer to that is relatively simple. Growing takes time because development isn't an instant process. For anyone who's thinking this is becoming a "how to grow an herb garden book", it's not. Growth isn't only with plants. It can be with people, ideas, animals, and even structures. Think about it. Babies take approximately nine months to develop in their mother's womb because they need time to develop. Cars need to be put on the production line to finally get on the road because you can't drive a car without it having all the necessary parts in it. If you drive a car without wheels, or an engine, or a steering wheel, or awesome music to blast through the speakers, there's something seriously wrong with your vehicle. Growing takes time, and it's within that time that the growth is crucial.

"Sometimes it's not the destination but the journey
that matters most."

Often, we try to speed up the process by doing things we think will benefit the production and development. In the end, we need to give it time. Waiting can be the hardest thing for a person. We wait to go to the bathroom, wait in traffic, wait to get medical results. But if you do wait and remain patient, it will all be worth it in the end.

Technology is continually changing around us. As soon as I got my iPhone 6, I was informed that the 6 plus was out. Then a few days later, the 6s plus and now there's an iPhone 11 Pro. Technology is truly a work of genius, making our world a faster place. It seems now that everything has become a race. Even at school, I see my classmates compete with each other as to who can do the least amount of work in the slowest time (which is also seen in more places than you think). I also see my best friends competing for who can hand up a project in the shortest amount of time. And sometimes when we see these things happening, we get all caught up in it and decide to participate in a race that isn't ours to run. The world is becoming a faster place. One hundred years ago, if you wanted to send a picture to the opposite side of the world, it would take over a week to get it there. But now, you can easily communicate with anyone, at any time of day. It's both amazing and discouraging. People get caught up in the race and compete for no apparent reason, only to compete. This drive is healthy, but also very dangerous. We need to be more careful out there and see what we are racing towards and why we are racing towards it.

Interrupting someone is so easy for some people yet incredibly hard for others. Voicing your opinions is hard to do when someone is overbearing, however interrupting someone is still rude. There will always be someone in your life that is overly talkative, and look like they need to take a long, deep breath and slow down. It reminds me of *Ace Ventura*, a movie about a pet detective. He would take a large breath in and then let out all the information that proved he was right in the end. When talking to these sorts of people, knowing how to get your point across can be hard. However, you don't necessarily need to interrupt them full on. When people are taking too long, think about why they are taking too long.

What can you do to say something in the conversation? For example, they might be rambling on about something. However, you could "interject" them to get your point across. Now you may be thinking, "what is wrong with the author? Is he serious about what he is saying?" Interrupting someone (only when you need to) is okay, but you need to know how to interrupt them. If you do it abruptly, you will probably get a death stare and another speech about interrupting people. However, if you interrupt politely, such as "clearing your throat" or starting with "excuse me, but …" or "I'm sorry, but…", it dramatically changes the situation. Waiting for the person to finish is the far better option. That way, you minimise the chance of confrontation.

Life can be very daunting as a teenager. We should put more value on the time we have. You see people dying in movies and their lives flashing before their eyes. They see all their family and friends, memories of a day far from the other year. Things like that probably do happen. Of course, I wouldn't know as I have never been on my death bed before. However, movies like these should get you thinking about how valuable time is and that we need to appreciate it.

"You don't know what you have until it is gone."

Appreciating time isn't something we do until we don't have it anymore. You remember all the time you spent with a best friend as soon as they betray you or you get into a fight. It has happened to all of us at some stage in our lives. Many people would deny it, but we have all lost someone close to us. Either to another person, to another job, to another country, to another social group or even to death itself. But we need to know that there is something better on the way. In the meantime, we need to be patient and wait for a brighter tomorrow.

Timing in life is essential. Without it, many things wouldn't function properly. Now what I am going to say next will turn your world upside down if you have read the entire chapter without being too impatient to skip to the end and find out the guts of it.

You need to be impatient.

Wait.

Let me rephrase that...

You need to wait, ready to strike. If you wait too long and are overly patient, you will miss your destiny. It's hard to tell when to take hold of an opportunity, but when the time comes, you will know if your timing was right or not. I will use the same example I used at the start. Cooking. If you leave the cake in the oven for too long, it will get burnt and probably taste horrible (it's either the timing or you're simply a terrible cook). If you wait too long, you miss your divine destiny and what you are meant to be and do. It's like a skeleton on a couch of a woman's house. "Ten minutes, she said. I'm just doing my makeup, she said". That's not to say that you need to be impatient either. You need to know when your time is and how you will react when your time comes. Always remember that you have a choice. Making the right choice is crucial to not only your world but the world of the people around you.

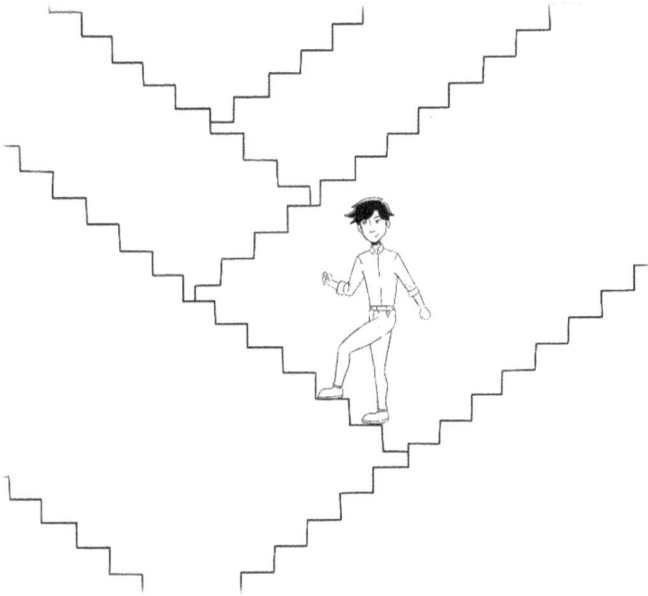

CHAPTER 3: THE ONLY WAY IS UP

Life always seems to throw you a curveball at the most unexpected moments. It could be the loss of a loved one, the loss of a job, or even the loss of a particular object that you are fond of. When these times come, people hit rock bottom and don't know what to do next. People begin to feel broken and hopeless, believing there is nothing worse that can happen in their lives. You may be reading this book right now in the hope that there is still something or someone out there that can improve your current circumstances. Well, there is. Many people make drastic decisions based on a single set back in their lives, thinking that the world is over. You see in the movies when they say, "it can't get any worse", it begins to rain, or in some way gets worse. Especially with teenagers, setbacks are dramatic. When a girl gets dumped out of nowhere, they instantly go into hibernation and become the worst person to be around. When a guy gets rejected by a sports team that he had dreamt of being in, the world comes crashing down around him. You see, when these sorts of things happen, reality hits us right in the face. It is at these times that we need to understand that the only way is up.

Positivity is hard to come by in this day and age. When I was in primary school, my teachers began to implement a concept called "bounce back". For each letter in "bounce back", there was a statement about getting back up from a fall. Unfortunately, it was incredibly dull by the time you got to the "u", so here it is in a nutshell. As soon as you are knocked down, you need to shake it off and get back up. My year six teacher gave me an example where a sick horse was put in a well to be buried. With each shovel of dirt that was thrown at the horse, he just shook it off and stepped up. By the time all the dirt was in the well, the horse was on top of it, fully healthy. That's the thing with setbacks. When an obstacle is in your way, you can use it to slingshot you forward. A simple phrase frequently used is how "a setback is a setup for a comeback". You need to understand that things will get better in your future. If people throughout history got discouraged like that, nothing would ever be achieved. We shouldn't only go through the hard times; we need to grow through the hard times.

"Happiness can be found, even in the darkest of times, if one only remembers to turn on the light." – Albus Dumbledore

Hope can always be found in the most unexpected places. When you hit your personal rock bottom, you need all the hope you can get. In your future, you can expect great things. Go out in your day expecting greatness. Love can always be found in the people around you, and there is still someone who loves you. It could be your spouse, your family, your friends, your co-workers, even your pets. Regardless, you are always loved through life. Even though you may feel like you have no one, you are truly loved. You are never alone in life because you always have God and His eternal love. You can never get away from that. But that's something saved for a further chapter.

You should expect great things in your future. If you go out with greatness in mind, you will receive it. Having an expecting mindset helps you understand that there are better things in your future. Next time you wake up, expect your day to be brighter than your yesterday. It can only get better from here.

I believe that friends are the family you choose. Friends are the people you want to be around who support and care for you. But the difference between family and friends is that you're stuck with your family for life. When you have hit rock bottom, you feel that you need someone to pick you back up. Sometimes, it's hard to find someone who will support you in your time of need. There is always someone who will pick you back up. Your family will be there to support your choices. If not them, your friends will still help you with whatever you might be going through. Now you may be saying, "Scott, my family doesn't support me like they used to, and I don't have any friends that are prepared to help me. What do I do?" You need to stop looking down and start looking up, because God will always pick you back up. He has been with you since the day you were born, and He will always be with you until the day you see Him again. You are never alone, not even on the inside. When you put yourself out there, you will find that there are people for you, the right people to lift you up and support you when you need them most.

Reaching out for help is hard for many people. Sometimes, people are too proud to admit that they need help, and unfortunately, those people need help the most. Seeking help from other people can be a hard process to go through. Here are some tips about getting through your pride and reaching out for help.

- First, you need to accept the issue or problem you might have. Understand that other people have the same problem as you. Not many people can safely say that they have an addiction or a problem. You need to accept yourself for who you are, faults and all.

- Second, evaluate how you got to where you are and why you have this problem. An important step in this is not blaming other people for your problems. That doesn't solve anything. You want to question yourself as to how you got where you are.

- Third and finally, be brave enough to put your hand out and seek help. Talk to someone. Speak out. Google is a fantastic tool, and you can use the internet to find helplines or websites that can help. This is only if you really want to change.

Guidance is something that people can either accept or decline. Sometimes we need guidance from whoever may offer it. People go through life not knowing what to do or how to do it. Everyone's life is in the hands of God. If you don't know who God is, I highly suggest you go out, get yourself a bible and pray about it. You could also visit your local church as they would be happy to help.

A man walks along the beach with God. The man looks back

and only sees one set of footprints in the sand. He asks God, "why have you not walked with me when I needed you in my life?" God replies, "I have not walked with you, but instead, I have carried you through all your life". The footprints the man was looking at were not his own but the footprints of God instead. If you don't quite understand this, to put it simply, God is carrying you all the way through life. And when you have hit rock bottom, know that He is there with you, getting ready to lift you back up.

Growth can only be achieved with time. But it is in the hard times that we grow the most. Take muscles, for example. When you are working out, your muscles are put under pressure. And when you stretch your body, your muscles stretch with you. Your muscles grow only because they are stretched and pressured. We are like a muscle and life is like a weight. When life pushes down on us, we stretch and contract. But when we come out of those hard times, we are stronger, smarter, and better off. The hard times are vital for our growth and because of it, we learn how to appreciate the easy times. When you go through a break-up, you get to understand a whole new form of emotions, which makes you appreciate the good times more. When you get rejected from a sports team, you know that you can better yourself for something greater than what you imagined before. The hard times shouldn't break us in life. They should make us.

When you stretch before you go for a run, you prepare yourself for the stress and tension your muscles will face. Use the hard times of life to your advantage. When we go through the hard times of life, we shouldn't complain or procrastinate, thinking we are the worst-off person in history. The hard times are like a sharpening block, meaning that when we go through them, we are shaper than we were before.

Valleys are created when two mountains sit next to each other, and the gap between them is at ground level (or at least close to ground level). The point of that fact is that you may be in a valley right now. You may be thinking "why can't I be on top of the mountain? Why do I have to be stuck in this valley?". Here is some news you might not expect: there is nothing wrong with being in the valley. Things don't grow on top of the mountains; they grow down in the valleys. This is a fact. The water from the top of the mountains naturally flows down into the valley where there is more oxygen for the plants, animals and humans to breathe. Therefore, things grow better in the valleys than they do in the mountains.

I attended the Catholic Youth Festival at the end of 2015, where one of the speakers was talking about his experience on Mount Everest. He was saying that mountains are the closest point to heaven and that he once hallucinated on top of a mountain that he saw his grandmother. He exclaimed to his climbing partner what he had just seen only to receive a reply "how's your granny doing?". It, of course, made the audience laugh because of the humour around it. But you see, experiences like that aren't only found in the mountains. The valleys of life are just as important as seeing your grandmother on Mount Everest. Take a breath and take a step back from it all. That's why the valleys are so crucial in life.

Light is more apparent in the dark, and sometimes you find yourself in the dark parts of life. But there is always a light at the end of the tunnel. The other day I was watching *Finding Nemo*. I got to the part where Marlin and Dory were at the bottom of the ocean, and Dory thought Marlin was her conscience. Marlin asked Dory what she saw. Dory replied, "I see a light". This light only turned out to be the light of a deep-sea angler fish that tried to eat them, but the scene where they are travelling towards the light assists my point. When we hit rock bottom in life, we are more attracted to our goals and our dreams. This is why we can't afford to give up on what is right in front of us. We need to go into our darkness and find the light at the end of the tunnel. Now in most cases, it won't be an angler fish that will try to eat you. Seek the light and don't be afraid of it. Some people are scared to get back up and out in life, living in fear of being hurt again. Have the courage to say that you've learnt from that experience, and it won't keep you from your destiny.

Pandora is a jewellery line that most countries have. It is super expensive and rather prestigious in my personal opinion. But I won't bother talking about that because there is a more promising story that I wish to tell. It is the myth of Pandora. Said to be the first woman of earth, Pandora was created by the Greek god Hephaestus and long story short; she received a box which she was not allowed to open under any circumstances. Compelled by her natural curiosity, she opened it and let out all the monsters of the world like sin, hate, murder, and so on. She tried to close the lid but failed to do so. After everything had been let out, the only thing left was hope. Now after telling you this story, don't be afraid to open a box of chocolates that are a moment on lips but a decade on the hips. Pandora's story is one that we can learn from. It shows us that at the end of the day, when we have been through hell and back, there will always be hope for us. We may not be able to see it at the moment, but it is there, waiting for us to seek it out. Only when we seek hope can we have the power to stop all the monsters of the world from feeding on us and using us. I quite like imagining Pandora's story and enjoy the many interpretations of it. But what I value most of all is the lessons it teaches. I also urge you to understand that curiosity is like a spark amongst the hay. If not treated with caution, you could burn down the barn.

Perspectives are powerful things and can be used to turn any situation around. I was looking through some old photos when I came across an optical illusion. It showed a young woman looking away but at the same time, an old woman with a large nose, wearing a bandana. Not many people can agree on what they see, so I encourage you to look at the image for yourself. You can type into your search engine, "young woman old woman optical illusion". It should come up with an image quite peculiar. The point is, we need to go through life choosing to see the best of it, no matter what. Through the ups, the downs, the turns and curves. And that is no different to the person in the room next to you. It is how we see things that ultimately impacts how smoothly we cruise through life. Some perspectives have much power behind them. Being around people with these perspectives allows you to see how they see partially. The point is, be careful what lens you look through in life.

Attitude also contributes to how you go through life. Turning setbacks into setups for comebacks can be quite hard to do if you don't have the correct attitude in mind. Having laser focus and the right inspiration helps as they drive us and our morals. Looking at setbacks differently is quite tricky if you are set in your ways. People might look at having a car crash as a blessing. The typical person will see it as a burden. It's all about how you view every single situation in life that determines how you will spend it. If you focus on the negatives and mope around all the time, you are immensely more likely to live a negative life with things that will only cause your frown marks to become deeper. But if you focus on the positives and are enthusiastic about your passions, you can expect to have a life that will challenge that perspective all the time.

Being a happy chappy 24/7 is quite a heavy burden to bear, but with the right inspiration, anything is achievable. Knowing this could be the difference between succeeding in life and not accomplishing anything. At school, it is just the same. As soon as I am given work, I look at how it can benefit me in the future and how I can use it to my advantage (even if I may never use the Pythagoras theorem ever again). That is my perspective compared to the typical two other ones. The first one is the perspective of the overachiever. This one involves them receiving the assignment and seeing what they need to do to smash out an A quadruple plus. Then the second one is the perspective of the slacker. Where they receive the assignment, put it in their bag and continue their conversation about their weekend. Although not all perspectives are like this, be careful as to how you see a challenge. Do you see it as a tombstone, or as a steppingstone to something greater?

Visualising where you want to go is vitally important in life. If you don't, how do you know what direction you're headed in? Usually, teenagers aren't incredibly concerned with their future. I'm majorly talking about young teens because when I look at some older teens, they're either super stressed out or know where they want to go. Knowing the right direction can be the difference between walking to success or walking to failure. Your environment is vital in understanding the direction you are headed in. You must know where you are now and where you want to go in future. When you see your reward and the steps to get you to your reward, you are more likely to take those steps and change any part of your plan depending on what your circumstance is.

"If you fail to plan, you plan to fail."

Having some idea of your goals and future is crucial in actually achieving something in life. Too many times, I come across kids who say to me that the only reason I do well in class is that I try, and they don't (which is pretty accurate). But that is only because they don't see the opportunity of what we are doing. As I reach yet another year in my education, I see how what I have learnt in the previous year helps me in my future years.

People in your life will come and go. A friend that you talked to nearly every day doesn't speak to you anymore. You change jobs because of someone you thought you wanted to be with, only to find that they belong to someone else. But the people who stick with you through thick and thin are the ones where you can find hope. We all need hope in our lives. Surrounding yourself with these kinds of people is something that we should all strive to do. Faith is another place where hope is derived. Although many people have lost their faith in their lives, it isn't hard to find it again.

Hope is something that we all need. When we lose that hope, what are we left with? Nothing! We don't have anything if we don't have hope. It doesn't have to be a considerable amount. It could be a hope that my food doesn't go too cold while I'm taking care of something else. It could be a hope that it rains tomorrow. At the same time, it could be as big as hope that I will wake up tomorrow, hope that my parents don't get divorced, hope that I can find someone who will give me a heart transplant. We all need hope.

CHAPTER 4: STANDING UP FOR STANDING OUT

With the population of earth being approximately 7.7 billion people, there is bound to be someone exactly like you, right? Unfortunately, no. There is no one else like you out there in the world. You are unique in your own way. The way you wake up is completely different from how your neighbour wakes up, or how the person in the next suburb wakes up because there is no one in the world like you today or ever. You are different because of the way you think, act, feel, react, speak, breathe, laugh, sing, dance, write and everything else you do. Without you, many plans wouldn't have been made, things wouldn't have been said or done, and the world would have changed entirely. Someone may laugh the same way you do or wear the same clothes as you do or heaven forbid, like the same person you have a crush on. But they aren't you. They have their own quirks and differences that are unique to them. For that reason, they have different burdens and blessings than you do.

Destiny is said to link us all together. In ways you don't understand, you are probably intertwined with the person sitting right next to you (which may be a real worry depending where you are reading this). And because of destiny, there is only one of you. People might look completely identical and have never even met before. The thing is, they are different from each other. There are over 70 trillion gene combinations (give or take a few hundred billion) that exist in the known world. This is far more than the people on earth. Logically, you are bound to be different than anyone in the world. Another main difference between people is their situation. No one in this world can say that their situation is the same as you because it isn't. You might have similar experiences, but you will never have the same circumstances as someone else, which is quite an important thing to remember. You were created for a specific purpose. People call it destiny, fate or fortune. Either way, there is and can only ever be one of you. If there were someone else exactly like you, you wouldn't be needed, or they wouldn't be needed. The point is: you are unique. I know a lot of people say it, but the first step in this chapter is understanding it.

Thinking for yourself is something that we get to do once we understand the world around us. My baby niece is already thinking for herself, and she isn't even two years old yet. We all have freedom of choice. We were all raised differently and therefore have different sets of morals. You know at a young age that tantrums will get you attention, but not much else. And you wouldn't throw a tantrum in your workplace at the age of 25, would you? You wouldn't because you choose not to (or you decide to throw a tantrum in your own way). Nevertheless, we have different yet similar morals to each other. When you begin to see and listen to other people's morals, you may even change your own. But the only reason you can do that is that you have the freedom to do so.

"What about twins?" you may ask, "aren't they the same?". Well, they aren't. Twins aren't the same. They may look identical, have the same clothes, same phone, same hair, but at the end of the day, they are different. Their brains are separate from one another. They do share a bond as many siblings do, whether it be through love and nurture or sibling rivalry. When we talk about twins, we usually think of identical twins, but that isn't always the case. Other sorts of twins happen like twins that may not necessarily look the same but are different genders, or have different physical features.

Along with being a human being, God gave us each a brain. As we think differently, we can learn differently as well. For example, there is usually a "smart one" in the family. Then you have the not so intelligent, the caring one, the tough one and then a few others. This can also occur in friendship groups. We all have neurological pathways in our brain that open when we discover something new. And because twins don't share one mind, they act, react, learn and live differently to each other and everyone else.

Opinions should often be kept to their own brain, but unfortunately, there is always someone in our lives that speaks the first thing that comes into their head. That may not always be a good thing. However, it may not always be a bad thing either. When you are the same as everyone else, you wear the same clothes, like the same music and do the same activities, you become disposable.

Think about it this way. When you apply for a job, you are looking for ways you are different from the crowd. If you are the same as everyone, you become expendable. The person hiring you sees he has eight pawns on his desk of portfolios, ready to march off into battle. They have highly similar credentials, and all say the same thing. Also, let's call the person hiring the king and queen. Then on the chessboard, you have the rooks, the knights and the bishops who stand right beside them. These are the people you would want to hire because they differentiate themselves from the pawns. When you are like the standard pawn in any industry, you are instantly disposable. That's why the pawns are up the front. But when you show that you are different, you immediately reach the end of the board and turn into something that is much more important and less disposable than a simple pawn.

Accomplishing goals at work or school is vitally important in showing your peers and superiors that you aren't as disposable as they might have previously thought. "But how do I do it" you may be asking. Well, I'm going to give you three simple tips that can dramatically improve your standing-out-ness (a word made by yours truly).

The first tip is about attitude. The attitude you bring into an environment immediately impacts your reaction to any situation that may come your way. If you are negative, then you won't be able to effectively respond to stress. Go to school or work with a positive attitude, choosing to see the best in every situation.

The second tip is to organise. Making yourself organised at school or work can be quite tricky in this day and age. Fortunately, you have a mobile device with you that can help. There are hundreds if not thousands of apps that you can install to keep you up to check with workloads that need to be completed or places you need to be.

Third and final tip, read the rest of this book. It's filled with even more strategies that will blow your mind and leave you wondering why you hadn't realised it before. But the point is, you should strive to stand out wherever you are.

Narrow is the road to success. When you begin on this road, you will face many trials and trepidations before you reach your goal. For example, learning to swim. For those who don't know how to swim, and you are over the age of 20 years old, I would urge you to at least try to learn how. Back to the point, when learning how to swim, you could have three experiences. The first experience is putting on your training floaties, ready and eager to learn. Next, you could be scared to go in the water without your floaties. And third, you swallowed way too much pool water because you didn't have your floaties when you jumped in. The last two can be considered obstacles. Often people talk about how the path to heaven is narrow and full of bumps, yet the path to hell is wide and straight. The point is, you will be tempted to put those floaties back on and take the wide, straight road. But have faith, persevere, and begin to see your obstacles as steppingstones instead of tombstones. Only then will you achieve more than anyone could have ever imagined you would accomplish. Keep your head above the water, floaties on the bench and just keep swimming.

Destiny pulls us together and pushes us apart as you probably already know by now. As we are all important in the grand scheme of the world, our circumstances need to be tested for us to maintain this difference. Connecting with other people through actions or sounds is one of the main ways we are important. If that doesn't make sense, think about a choir. Not a whole symphony or a band. Just a choir. When they harmonise with each other, they all need to sing a different note, or a group of them sings one note and the others sing another. If someone doesn't hold up their note, they ruin the sound. When they all have different notes that are properly harmonised, they are all critical to the intended sound of the song.

What about you? What makes you so different that you can't be disposed of or replaced? Everyone has something about them that makes them different. Some people go through life without knowing what that is. Go out and find what makes you different. It might be your family, your passions, your skills. Knowing this is the difference from being a pawn or a king (or a queen).

Skill is something we all have. If you can play an instrument, that is a skill. If you can draw, that is a skill. If you can make, create, destroy, see, hear, show or do something, that is a skill. Even thinking is a skill, so you can't say that you don't have one at all. You need to use as many of your skills as you can. Too often, I come across people that have the potential to be so much more than they are, but they neglect their skills to fit in with society. And to all you people out there who are doing that, I ask, why? Why you would want to be disposable, the same as everyone else and mediocre? There is nothing you can do about being unique and different. Why waste that talent? I might be a bit harsh, but what's wrong with you? You are given this skill or passion to show the world. It says in the bible that you don't put a lamp under a bowl, you put it on a stand so that it can shine its light all through the house (Matthew 5:15). Choose to be on the stand and not under the bowl.

Ideas are beautiful things. They can give a community hope, uplift people, bring people together and make the world a better place. But at the same time, they can be used for the wrong reasons, the complete opposite. Being in a team, you need to use that brain of yours to think of brand spanking new ideas that will change the world. Think about a chair. Each leg of a chair represents a person. When a chair leg is slightly shorter, the chair becomes more susceptible to breaking when weight is placed on it. When you don't play your part in a team, when you neglect your skills, when your opinion is not taken into account, when you don't have any ideas or don't contribute to that group, you are like the short leg. Eventually, that team will experience weight; weight and stress that will break it apart, and you will be replaced. I heard once that a team is only as strong as its weakest person, and I'm sure you don't want to be the weakest person in the team. Or is it okay for you to be the one that isn't noticed, not saying anything or making your point count?

No!

It's not okay.

There are too many people out there who are afraid to speak out. Changing this may not be instant but make an effort to put yourself out there. You need to show the world what you're made of because you are destined for greatness.

New ideas come from new thinking. If you think about it, innovation means new thinking and new ideas. No one would change if everyone was the same. If no one changed, no one would ever change, and everyone would be the same. But thank God that He put adventure in us. He gave us curiosity and wonder. You need to understand that you aren't a robot. You have the power to think and discover new things. Creativity and imagination cannot be reproduced and replicated. There's an example every week you can plainly see. Look at the music charts this week. In the following days, look at it again. Is there a difference? There is a difference because people are continually coming up with new ideas, new concepts, and new ways to express themselves. The world is truly a magnificent place, but we wouldn't know that unless we change, unless we sought to do something that hasn't been done before. We need to aim for that every day. We need to wake up and say to ourselves that we will achieve new standards today. We will do the impossible, and we will overcome our obstacles. Picking up this book and coming this far is a clear example of new thinking in progress. You were intrigued by this book, and for that, you are reading it right now. I urge you to be open to new experiences and make the most of every day.

Creativity and bravery to express it are two completely different things. Out of the ten people that want to write a book, only one person actually does (approximately). And for all those people who are famous now for whatever reason, they are because they embraced their passion, talents and skills, and chose to have an innovative mind. Back in year 7, I completed a report of the migration from Africa and focused on how the simple caveman had an innovative mind. I did an entire stop motion video showing his brain growing and thinking new thoughts that had never been thought before his time. Looking back at it now, if you don't have an innovative mind, you're no better than a caveman. Choose to have an innovative mind and don't get all caught up in the rush of the same old boring schedules. However, there is a difference between being irrational and being logical. If you have an innovative irrational mind, you might say, "I'm going to wake up on a cloud tomorrow and ride my pretty, pink pony to work". An innovative logical mind might say, "when I get up tomorrow, I'm not going to lose my temper on the way to work in traffic, and I am going to go to work with an uplifting attitude". Choose to have a logical, innovative mind and make every thought count.

Jesus Christ, Rosa Parks, Malala Yousafzai. What do these three people have in common? They stood up for standing out. They said no to the people who said they couldn't do something, and they spoke up for their morals and beliefs.

Take the story of Rosa Parks. It was February 4, 1913. It was a typical day in the city of Montgomery, Alabama. But it wasn't for Rosa Parks. She refused to give up her seat to a white person on the bus. Her one act of standing up (or rather sitting down) for what she believed in changed the entire world as we know it. She enforced change just by choosing to sit down. How much more change can you make by standing up?

Now let's travel to middle eastern Europe where Jesus Christ of Nazareth brought forth the truth of God and created Christianity. As He was given divine knowledge and a message from God, it didn't matter that people looked down on him and judged him for doing good. He enforced a positive change in the world on a major scale and changed the history of humanity as we know it.

Now the final example of Malala Yousafzai. In 2012, she stood up for education for young girls and was critically injured because of it. But she emerged a leader of a new age of education for all girls. She won a Nobel peace prize in 2014 and achieved so much because she stood up for her passion and for what she believed in.

I urge you to have the same courage and stand up for what you believe in.

Perseverance is key when standing up. For some, physically standing to their feet is a struggle. For those who have something to say but are afraid to, the struggle is felt much the same. When you venture towards your goal of standing up, you will experience many trials. These trials may include (but aren't limited to) critique from people around you, challenges you must overcome and things you must do and say that will prove your point. For those people who have something to say, you need to keep with it. You need to see your goal and run towards it. Don't let anyone or anything stop you. If it is meant to be, then it will be.

However, you may be running in the wrong direction. Before you travel towards your goal, ensure that it's what you truly desire. Not what your friends want, not what your parents want, not what society expects of you. It needs to be what you want. And by the end of it, hopefully, you will know that all the blood, sweat and tears will have been worth it because you made a difference. In the three examples of successful people who stood up for standing out, they were all faced with decisions, temptations and obstacles that they could have given into to make the journey easier for them. But because they persevered, they achieved great things and made their impact on the world we know today. Their influence is a direct result of their difference, knowing that no one would ever be like them.

Achieving your goals doesn't happen overnight. No one really knows when they will achieve their goal and make their full impact on the world. Only God knows. We need to be brave enough to acknowledge that our story has already been written. When we do stand up, we need to do so for the right reasons. When people are driven by the wrong motives such as revenge, vengeance, a person they are around or even their own sub-conscious, then they are different for all the wrong reasons. Look at all the world wars and great wars through history. In the first and second World War alone, there were over 90 million deaths and countless more injuries. Because of the war, people now know the name "Hitler". He did make his impact on the world, but not for the right reasons. Knowing that you are going to do something to change the world is amazing. Knowing you're standing up for the right reasons is even greater because you know that what you are about to do, what you have done, or what you are currently doing will change the lives of many people for the better. Use your skills, pursue your passions and make sure you are different for the right reasons. Stand up for standing out.

CHAPTER 5: BIRDS OF A FEATHER

Birds of a feather flock together. Think about it. Look at your friends. How did you become the way you are with them today? Was it because you shared a similar interest, or you enjoy the same hobbies? That's exactly my point. This is especially evident at school. Every day, I see all different types of groups. The troublemakers, the soccer kids, the not so popular kids, the Asians, the Aussies, the nerds, the geeks, the so-called "cool kids" and then there are some other neutral groups. People often search for others similar to themselves or who they see themselves in. In an environment like school or work, people want to feel safe and accepted in their peer group. But if you start to realise that you're different from your group, things begin to change. You begin to act differently when you're around them, trying to fit in with a group you don't belong in. Luckily, there is always a group for you. Often it takes a while to find that group, and you may go through many others to find it. But there is always light at the end of the tunnel and hope that you can be comfortable with who you are.

Sharing is caring. With some things yes, but not all things, of course. If you share the flu, that's not caring. If you share a spouse or significant other, that's definitely not caring. Why is it that people share their bad habits with others? This sharing is not caring either. When you're around the wrong type of people, they begin to share bad habits with you.

Bad habits come from bad people. This may be a bit harsh, but in reality, it's brutally true. When you are around your friends, co-workers and even enemies, you change and adapt yourself to the needs and wants of others by sharing their traits to fit in. This ties in with peer pressure, which will be further expanded on in a later chapter. Think about your own habits. Where did you learn this, or why do you do that, or when did you begin that habit? By looking at these types of questions and applying them to your own lives, you can see which friends, enemies or general people you shared the habit with. Habits are very dangerous things if they are negative and wrong. Be aware of your habits and where you share.

Judging people is not right. Rating people on what I like to call "the human scale" isn't too bad, however. Everyone has a number in life. It can range from 10 to 1. However, as I said before, ranking people is not right. But rating yourself is a highly beneficial way to see where you can improve. If you can say what number you are, let me fix it up to improve your accuracy. You can never be exact, as you are always changing because the world is ever-changing. Rating yourself helps you become a better person because if you know where you are wrong, you can see more opportunities to grow. Take a moment to look at you. Just you and only you. Not your family, your friends, your pets, just you. Think about your habits and what your "daily routine" actually is. Is it a healthy routine, like exercising, making conversation with friends or experiencing new things? Or is it something that is not healthy like smoking, using vulgar language frequently or having a negative look at life. I want you to write down as many habits as you possibly can. Looking at all of your habits, try to rate yourself again and make sure to be as honest with yourself as you can. Whatever number you choose, make sure that you are telling the truth. How you see yourself directly impacts the way others see you.

Question: What number are you? You may think it's your age, or your IQ, or the amount of Facebook friends you have or Instagram followers.

What did you rank on the human scale?

Was it a 10 out of 10? Well, it wasn't because no-one is perfect, let's get that out of the way. But more realistically, was it around the 7 mark. If so, good job. Gold star. Give yourself a pat on the back. Just remember to be humble about it. No one likes arrogance even though you're "clearly a 9 and a half". But that's beside the point.

You need to be 100% truthful to yourself when you are ranking yourself. Now, as previously said, you shouldn't rate others. However, being aware of what "number" people are isn't a bad thing either. When you are truthful with your ranking, you need to take into consideration your attitude and maturity. These two factors mess up your entire outlook on life. I see so many of my classmates that have the wrong attitude and low maturity level yet have the capability to be a straight-A student, instead of a big pain in the A. For all those kids and everyone else out there who think it's cool if you act dumb just to fit in, what on earth are you doing? Eventually, the attention you crave won't be given to you. And then what will you do?

Observing what you see around you and who is around you is important in understanding where you belong (or at least where you want to belong). Often people see what they want to be but fail to recognise where they are. Because of this, they can't reach their goal. It's like a child that wants to go to Disneyland but doesn't realise it's on the other side of the world. It is often quite challenging to surround yourself with 10's and not 2's. Expecting that you can easily fit in with a 10 if you are only a 5 is a big leap, but it is still good thinking. You need to expect big things; that is healthy for a positive mindset. However, if you expect too big of a thing (and yes, "thing" is the correct term), you may get overwhelmed. You must try to surround yourself with people of a higher level than you. On a side note, when you "rate" other people, don't do it from a biased point of view, that won't get you anywhere. Having genuine 10's in your life can dramatically affect the way you behave, think, act, speak and anything else you do. You are like the people you hang around. I will probably mention this several more times through this chapter so bear with me. You need to choose to be around positive people.

Negative people attract other negative people and therefore, negative vibes. There will always be negative people out there. You may not know it or notice them in your life, but they are there. It may be a relative, a partner, a friend, a work colleague or even you. If it is, don't stop reading now. When negative people are around you, they automatically bring the general vibe of a space down. When they begin to talk, it's like poison or a virus in the human body. It begins to take hold of whatever is close to it and corrupts it. This is how bad habits are born, and although you may not think of it as a bad habit, it really is.

Negative people are often oblivious to the nature of positive people, and although they say opposites attract, this is not the case. This has nothing to do with magnets that come together at the positive and negative poles at all. It all has to do with the way you think, act and behave. Negative people are not healthy for anyone, even themselves. In everyone's life, we all have some friends that won't stop talking or gossiping or being negative. The real fact is, you need those people but not in a way that you would expect.

Destiny is spelt with a total of 7 letters if you didn't know. But so is the word chicken. And believe me, you don't want to associate your destiny with people who seem like chickens. You need to strive to be with the eagles, soaring high above the clouds. The fact that there are chickens in your life is something to be worried about. But don't worry, you won't catch a disease but rather be changed in a way you might not like. Being cautious of these chickens in your life is crucial in knowing who the eagles are.

"You can't expect to soar with the eagles if you hang around with chickens."

You can't expect to be a better person if you frequently associate with corrupted people. Learning to fly with eagles takes time, but you must get through the tough times with the chickens first. Now you may be seriously feathered out by now, and I believe I am as well. But be cautious about the people you associate with. If you aren't careful, you might find yourself in the chicken coop instead of above the clouds where the eagles soar.

If you want to know what you are going to be like in the future, look at your friends. They usually reflect whoever you are in the future. Peer pressure is the primary catalyst of this reflection. Whenever people submit themselves to the commands of others, they are giving away their self-control.

Growing up, I was always the nice, polite kid that wouldn't say no to anything unless it was a clear violation of what I knew. This was three main things:

1. Nice

2. Nicer

3. Nicest

I was all about being selfless. Now when I look back, all I see are the many times I was used. It is a real pain because I know that I can't go back and change anything. That would be too dangerous. The point is, I was constantly refining myself and the people I associated with. I remember switching from up to 5 groups in one term until I finally found somewhere I sort of belong; a group where I didn't need to pretend to be something or someone else. Once you realise the people who you don't want to be like, you can change yourself.

Manipulative people are the absolute worst in life. They will tear you to shreds just to get something they want from you and then move on like you didn't mean anything. A word of warning for the future, treat these people with extreme caution. One wrong move could slide you into the rung of their ladder to supremacy. That sounds rather intense in my head and maybe yours as well.

Let me dull it down a couple of steps. Social climbers are the people who will use you to get ahead in life. You can see this almost everywhere in the world.

I've seen many people come and go through my life and I'm sure you will experience that too. It might be that new kid who talked to you and then suddenly stopped, that partner that lost interest in less than a month, or that fake friend who stabbed you in the back for a cut at the big leagues. The point is, you will see these people, and it's all about how you respond to them. Choose not to let yourself be used for the purpose of others. At the same time, don't be cruel and cold because those people aren't good either. You will learn what to be like and where you fit in overtime. That's what life does. It moves you and twists you until you're the perfect shape you need to be.

Groups change, people move on, and very few things stay the same. Finding where you fit in at school or work can be challenging to figure out. But you're not alone. Everyone is figuring themselves out. People always try new things, seeing if they like it or not, then either move on or stick with it. But that's how everything works, or more so how life works.

For example, what are your favourite hobbies? Now think about how you were when you first started that specific hobby. You tried it, and you thought, "wow, this is fun or interesting or amazing, I'm going to continue doing this as a hobby". Well, you probably didn't sound exactly like that, but it went along the lines of that. This is how we find what we like or where we belong. Go through some serious trial and error if you want to find out where you belong and what you like. Your results all boil down to your skills and maturity.

Where do you belong?

If you don't know or want to try something new, ask yourself three main questions. The first one is "<u>what am I doing?</u>". A simple question. By "what are you doing", I don't mean sitting on a chair or eating spaghetti or reading this book. I mean the job you have, the people around you, and what you enjoy doing. The second question is, "<u>am I happy with where I am?</u>". This is a simple yes or no. Your final question is "<u>what do I want to do and where do I want to go?</u>". This doesn't necessarily mean you answer with something like to the toilet or to bed. Once you answer these three questions, you can begin to change your life, so you can say "I am here, and I am happy".

Analysing people's behaviour isn't always the easiest thing to do. You may think someone is nice, but then you get to know them, and they're not. It's the same with you. If you are around people, they might be kind to you. But then once you bring someone else into the picture, they change their personality entirely. It's almost as if the person has a multiple personality disorder. Unfortunately, this is the case for many people which is in a chapter of its own. But for the meantime, lets understand the basics. Discovering the difference between your fake friends and your real friends is something people are seriously bad at doing, and they don't even know it. So, to everyone out there, no matter how perfect you think you are at judging people, first off, stop judging, and second, you're not perfect. No one is. Finding your real friends is important. You want to know you can rely on them in any circumstance because that's what friends are for. When you're with your friends, think about three things. Positivity, reliability and support.

- First, are they positive? Positive people are perfect pairs for other positive people (unnecessary alliteration but I digress).

- Second, have they been there for you in the past? Can you rely on them or not? Not to say that one let down means you dump them immediately, but are they likely to let you down again in the future?

- And third, do they make you want to become a better person? Do they see the best parts of you and rejoice? Do they see the worst parts of you and want you help you improve?

If you answered no for two or more of the questions, you might want to re-evaluate your relationship with them. For now, I leave you to figure the fakes from the reals yourself while I do the same.

Evaluating who you can and can't trust is important for finding who you want to be. But sometimes, you trust the wrong people and sometimes you don't trust the right people. How can you clear up this confusion?

Start with your attitude. Attitude is everything. If you "wake up on the wrong side of the bed", you tend to make decisions based on a negative point of view. If you found out you won the lottery, you will make decisions accordingly. Watch out for your attitude and whether you are controlling it, or other people and circumstances are. One of the most common things that people tend to do is allow their environment to control their attitude. But here's a little secret that shouldn't be a secret: people and circumstances can only control your attitude if you let them. You need to choose to stay positive and analyse your "trust circle" from a non-biased perspective.

Next, focus on your future. By this I mean how you see yourself in five or ten years down the road. Do you see yourself with this person or group of people? Have you noticed that they aren't in your life? You may not be a fortune teller, so I'll help you out with a crystal ball of prediction. Look at how they are now and make the decision based on what they could be in the future. Approximately 90% of people will keep their habits. It's the rare 10% that change.

Finally, understand that people change and therefore you will change. When you see who you can trust, be careful you aren't trusting the mask instead of the person behind the mask. But that's for another chapter.

Change is often rejected by people who hate it, which is most of the world. People are afraid of change, fearful of the confusion and what it can bring. When you try to soar with the eagles and get told that you don't belong above the clouds, it can hit people hard. Everyone goes through this; being told you don't belong somewhere or in a particular group. It's happened many times to me. Being rejected by eagles is hard, and you may believe that they are right. But in some cases, those people may be chickens trying to keep you down with them. These people often find joy in telling people they are wrong and that they don't belong. Have the courage to stand up to these people. Only when you do can you finally soar with the real eagles. It's basically a sign that you're getting there. When people say you can't, you don't, or you won't, then you must, you will, and you can (in the right contexts of course). I mean, if it clearly says on the box, do not shake, clearly don't shake it. This is only regarding people in the world. Please be realistic with this and keep it in context. When you are told to stay with the chickens, know that there's an eagle inside of you, just waiting for you to have the courage to set it free.

Maintaining a good group of friends can be hard to do. You're always changing, the world is always changing, and we are constantly finding out new things about people we have known for a long time. When people try to be around us that we consider a slightly lower number, what do we do? First off, don't send them away. If they want to be around you, it would be of great benefit to them. However, if you let them take advantage of you and bring you down, only then does it become an issue. Back to the point, I would encourage you to befriend people who might be a lower "number" than you. They want to grow just like you have. Birds of a feather flock together and people still finding themselves may come into your life only to leave you several weeks or months later. The only way you can let these people enter your life is by accepting them and understanding that once upon a time, you were in their position as well.

Friends are the family you choose. You may think your friends are the people you are stuck with or the people who just exist around you. But alas! You can choose who your friends are. That also means you can choose who aren't your friends. The people in your life that you don't want to be around are a touchy subject for everyone. That one person who wants to be your friend desperately but is "just weird". That girl who always sits next to you but kind of creeps you out. Or even that guy who always talks to you but is always negative. There will be many people you will see in life that you will want to avoid. Unfortunately, some of them don't want to avoid you. So, what do you do when you don't want to be with someone?

First off, you shouldn't judge them because of their physical qualities or appearance. Second, be sure of the decision that you want to make, and that the person is unhealthy for your life. Now thirdly, what to do. Not immediately, but distance yourself from that person bit by bit. I don't mean move to Antarctica and change your name. That's pushing it too far. You may start to hint to them that you might not want to be around them as much. Don't be mean, rude or insensitive. Be empathetic because you might also be the person that someone else wants to avoid. When you approach them, pay attention to them and take the time to speak with them. You may absolutely hate it, but it is essential for you. Once you understand their perspective, please let them down easy. Don't be cynical or rude; just tell them how you feel.

Keep refining yourself because birds of a feather flock together.

CHAPTER 6: HOW MUCH DOES THE WORLD WEIGH?

Earth: a planet inhabited with plants, animals and humans. It is the third planet from the sun and weighs 5.972×10^{24} kg (scientifically speaking). Our personal world can weigh far more than that. Think about your world. Think about your commitments, your family, your friends, your enemies, your habits and your life in general.

How much does the world really weigh? When you think about it, the world could weigh any amount for any person. For the more logical person, it will weigh approximately 5.972×10^{24} kgs based on scientific and mathematical logic. However, you can't solely base everything on that sort of reasoning. We aren't robots. We have hearts, brains and feelings. We make mistakes, and we act based on our emotions and what we believe to be true. Regardless, we do whatever we can to hold our world all by ourselves, and in the end, it will crush us.

In the 2015 movie *Home*, the aliens called "Boov" try to take over a world that wasn't theirs. This movie can also represent humans as well. We can be illogical and make irrational decisions based on what we are made to believe is right. When we find out we aren't, we will lie to ourselves and others. The point is, understanding how much your world weighs is the first step in understanding it.

The world can weigh any number of tonnes or kilograms (or pounds depending on what scale you use), but it doesn't matter because to you, it's your own world that matters the most. You may be concerned with the world of others. That friend you always want to impress, or that significant other you don't want to disappoint. Your world needs to matter the most. For now, let's focus on you and only you.

Finding how much your world weighs can be a difficult task. Be completely harsh but logical with yourself. If you weigh something with your hand or you put it half on the scale, you get an inaccurate measurement. I saw a video the other day of an old woman going on the scales. She was utterly shocked at her weight only to find out that her husband was stepping on the scale behind her. It made me laugh a little, but it made me think about how important this is. Not to say you should do this to your own partner, but should look at your world and see how much it weighs. There are no set measurements for this, so it's up to you to decide what is important. View your life as a weight on a scale. What number would you see?

Expectation is something we are all burdened with. The expectation to do the right thing when no one is around you, being kind to those who may not deserve it, or being on time for something. Why do we conform to some of these expectations? We have an obligation to some of the necessary things to do, however, the rest is different. The things we do to fit in and the pressure we undergo to look or at least seem "cool". Why are you holding this weight? It may be as simple as you want people to accept you, that you want to fit in or that you don't want to seem different because being different is dangerous. Fitting in can be difficult when you are so special and unique. And holding the weight of your world doesn't help your case. Instead, understand why you are holding up your world. You are only holding your world; not the world.

Controlling situations can be a dangerous game. People have sought power throughout the entire history of the world. Because of this, many people are corrupted and ruin the world around them for themselves and others. Some believe that controlling their situation means changing themselves to make others happy, providing an illusion of being in control. In reality, they are being controlled. We all have done it, and we may even continue to do it in future. Realising you are changing yourself for the benefit of others is the first step to breaking free. This reminds me of a song from Ariana Grande called Break Free. The chorus says, "this is the part when I say I don't want to, I'm stronger than I've been before". And she is 100% correct. Although you might think differently, the stage you are at right now is the strongest stage you have ever been at in life.

You shouldn't submit yourself to what other people want. It is good to find a compromise to a problem or see things a different way, but that doesn't mean you end up being the only one to change. These unnecessary changes mean you aren't living your life. Instead, someone or some people are living it for you. This is a common issue because people always want to be of a higher social status. I've seen some of my best mates turned to what I call "the dark side" because the wrong people have influenced them. And as you know, birds of a feather flock together. Why are you changing to make the wrong people happy?

Heavy is the burden of expectation. The more expectation you have, the more weight you need to carry. You may be carrying all of this weight alone, meaning it's even worse for you. When you let people control you, it's like adding 50 kg to your weight. And that is never a good thing. This reminds me of myself in so many ways. I used to go through my schooling wanting to impress someone else. Seeking approval and wanting to be recognised for what I can do and not so much for who I really am. Then I had a realisation. I finally understand now why I was so robotic (in a way). I would do the same things to impress or uphold the same expectations of people who didn't care. And through that part of my life, I didn't even know I was doing it. When I look back at myself, I begin to question my actions and the reasons behind them. The only way you can break from something is when you challenge it.

I saw an ad the other day that showed a man saying thank you to all the people who set rules in stone, who said you couldn't do something and said what was impossible. Without these people, we wouldn't have anything to question. This is the essence of how people who are trying to demote you can promote you instead. Controlling how you react to something is a two-way street. That is to say; you need to weigh up the emotions and facts to get the best possible outcome. Why are you carrying a heavy load?

Carrying expectation means you are trying to carry someone else's happiness. Many people have become numb to this in a way that they don't know they're doing it. You might be surprised whose happiness you are holding up. Some people lock their happiness onto you, forcing you to carry it as you do with everyone else. But at the end of the day, you are in charge of your own happiness. You don't have to worry about someone else's happiness because your own should be your primary concern. That's not to say that you become selfish and self-centred (that won't get you anywhere). It's more about understanding whose happiness you are holding and why you are holding it. You don't need to make other people happy. You can if you want to, but don't get all caught up in it. When you carry someone or want to carry someone, you are distracted from your own life. Be wary of this. Be self. Just self. Not selfish and not overly selfless. A sweet spot in the middle called self.

An atlas is a book of maps and charts. Have you ever wondered why it's called this? It's called an atlas because of the Greek titan named Atlas. After being on the losing side of the great titan war, Atlas was forced to hold the sky on his shoulders. Many myths and stories about Atlas have been created including how Perseus turned him to stone so he needn't worry about holding the sky. The point is, he was holding the world together, and because of that, the people and gods were happy. Do you think he was happy holding all their lives and being trapped forever, forced to carry the sky? Although this is all Greek mythology, it provides an important point. By holding the world for everyone else, you don't get to experience it yourself. The myth of Atlas means that you don't need to hold the world for everyone. Holding the world for everyone around you isn't an easy job.

Uplifting-people are some of the best people you can encounter in life. However, not everyone is uplifting and positive. Consider the grumpy guy in the cubicle next to you at work, the woman at the grocery store that gives you a sarcastic response to everything, or that sibling that exists for the gloom and doom. Everyone can be positive and uplifting for the people around them, but as soon as those specific few people aren't around them, their mood changes. You can see it with your friends, your family and even random people. When I'm with one of my best mates, they act a certain way. But when someone I don't usually associate with comes into the picture, both of our moods change (and sometimes I don't even know I'm doing it). But at the same time, you need to stop trying to make everyone else happy. You can't just live your life making everyone else happy because in doing so, your happiness is sacrificed. Be careful of who's world and happiness your holding.

Enjoying life is like watching your favourite movie. You have control of how you view the movie, but you can't control how someone else sees the film. I don't mean literally view it from a specific angle, but perspective and how they interpret it. Living your own life is entirely different from living someone else's life. Why live someone else's life when you have your own to live?

Think about your favourite dessert. It could be cheesecake, tiramisu, sticky date pudding, chocolate cake, fruit salad, whatever you like. Now think about someone else having it, and you take it. But when you do, you find that you no longer have your own. Life can sort of work like this. When you live someone else's life, you find that someone else has taken over yours. You have your own life to live, not somebody else's. Living in harmony with someone is different, and being a part of someone's life is still different. Many people confuse living someone else's life and living with someone else. How would you feel if someone just took your fried ice cream (my personal favourite) and you were left with nothing? The point is, you have your own life to live, and so does your spouse, your work colleague, your family and your friends. Just be yourself and live your life, because everyone else is taken.

New things never last. Lots of people try to keep things in new condition but eventually, they end up old. The "new" will always be replaced by the new yet again, making it old. The point is, things can never be kept in perfect condition. When they crack and brake, we panic sometimes. We fuss over the things that happen to us that we consider to be of high stress. It could be someone cutting you off in traffic, or giving you a bad look, or taking your car park. When we crack under pressure, what happens? Most of the time, we have a meltdown. Not like the Ice Age movie, but a mental meltdown or a panic attack. Building yourself back up from that again can be hard to do. It's not easy to build a house from a pile of bricks. When you crack under pressure because of a mistake you made, how do you feel? You feel like you have let everyone down and that you disappointed everyone. Yeah, well, you might have. But understand that no-one is perfect. If everyone were suddenly swallowed up by the earth because they did something wrong, we would all be in huge trouble. My point is, when you crack because you are maintaining everyone else's happiness, understanding that no one is perfect is a good thing. Now, you can make yourself better. You have a new beginning, a fresh start. That's not something you get every day. Take advantage of it because you may not get it again.

Controlling everything around you is impossible. It's like telling the sea to stop moving, the sun to stop shining or a child to stop growing. You can't have all the control in the world. You probably shouldn't because if one person runs the world, it would not be a very good place for everyone. But having control isn't a bad thing either. It's like a knife. If your hand starts creeping from the handle to the blade, you're going to get cut. That is to say: you need to be careful about the control you have, especially self-control.

Falling into the trap of self-superiority is dangerous. That may be where you are at right now. You can fix that by deciding not to be controlling and stuck up. That may offend all the stuck-up people out there, and that's understandable. But I won't dwell on that if you won't. To the point, having control is a great responsibility, because you are always stressed with decisions to make, things to approve, people to see, words to say and ways to act. You can have control but a measured amount of it. At the end of the day, God is in control. Some call it karma, others call it fate, and still, others call it destiny. But God is in control. He knows what's going to happen and what isn't, what you want to say but don't (or won't), and He understands where you are in life.

Divine guidance isn't something commonly experienced by everyone. For one thing, some people don't believe at all, so most of them are ruled out. They are probably the best people to seek guidance because they need it more than anyone else. Having God in control may seem scary because you don't know what is going to happen. It's like working on a group project. I recall an assignment that I had to complete with a group of people I didn't usually associate myself with, and so, I didn't know how they were going to work. I didn't know if they were no-workers, hard-workers, half-workers or just worked at all. This slightly scared me because the unknown is scary. But I had faith in my group. In the end, we got a pretty good mark (considering it was only year 7). We need to believe that things will change and that someone is watching over us. Although it's scary to think about how we don't know what is going to happen, it's exciting as well. My dad taught me when I was little that you shouldn't feel nervous about anything. The feeling of butterflies in your stomach is the same as the feeling of excitement and that you're eager for a new experience. Choose to be excited about what God holds for your today, your tomorrow and your forever.

Dangerous is the road of kindness and generosity. By this, I mean that being kind-hearted is very dangerous. Being too kind is not safe. Not being kind at all is even worse. But having a kind soul is important in life. Growing up, my objective was to hold everyone's happiness or at least make other people happy because they came first before me. But this went too far one day. I didn't realise what would happen when I woke up that morning. Okay, it's not that dramatic, but when I tried to stop my friend from getting hurt, in the process, I got hurt as well. And this didn't only happen once, but multiple times through my childhood. I would put myself in the firing line for others. It was just out of habit that I didn't want anyone to get hurt. When people did, I felt as though I had let them down. Further down the track, when starting high school, it was a completely different world for me. And people saw that I was nice. Nice to the point where it was a problem. Maybe not a problem but definitely something to look for and exploit. When I saw what had happened, I knew that something had to change. I was then never nice to anyone ever again. The end.

Nah, I'm just kidding! It's not that kind of story. I learnt what level of kindness I had to use. Not over, not under, but just right. Over my time, I have found that place where I can still be kind but not to the point where I can be taken advantage of. I could go on and on about my endeavours, but it's not about me, it's about you. Be careful about having a kind soul and find a place in the middle.

Kind-hearted people are probably the most "taken-advantage-of" people on the earth. That's usually because they are too kind to say otherwise. When society becomes manipulative and takes advantage of these people, they exploit their greatest weaknesses. It's like in a movie when the villain takes advantage of a random person who then either becomes the hero or helps the hero in some way. The point is, when people take advantage of you, you need to confront them. That's not to say knock them a new brain cell. Just talk to them. When people take advantage of you, don't seek revenge, because you only create a vicious cycle of hate and revenge. You need to choose to put an end to it. If you don't, it will get to a point where you ruin not only yourself but the people around you as well. I was once told that the best revenge is success.

The truth is: the world of every person can't be held alone. You can't expect to be the strongest person and keep the world together. You need help to hold the world. Everyone needs help because we all have our own problems. But at the same time, you can't let someone else carry your entire world. You have your own world to carry. You may not be superman, you may not be the hulk, and I definitely know you're aren't the terminator. When you hold your world, remember that the people around you are there to support you. It's like you are part of a table. And you are one of the legs. Without the others to help stabilise your top, your world will fall into pieces and break before your eyes. One way or another, you will get through life and hold the world above your head and say "I've done it. I hold my world in my hands". It's not only your hands but the hands of your parents, your siblings, your children, your friends, your spouse, your co-workers, people you don't even know and most importantly, the hands of God. So how much does your world really weigh?

CHAPTER 7: SOCIETY'S GREATEST FLAW

Expectations are all around us in life, coming from every angle. From friends, from parents, from teachers, from just about anyone that we come into contact with in our lives. These expectations can begin to control our lives and run it into the ground. What's really disturbing is that these expectations can even kill people, as they are dangerous in the wrong circumstances. Self-belief and self-view are what stand up towards peer pressure, which is the main idea of this chapter. The more expectations we bear, the more pressure we take on. Peer pressure is stronger in specific stages and places in our lives. For instance, peer pressure seems the strongest in the adolescent stage of our lives. It is during this time where our decisions are typically made based on our emotions and environment. Peer pressure is also strongest when we venture into a new challenge. We are constantly being influenced by people all around us. At school, in the workplace, on the street, at the shops, everywhere. It is up to us to stand up and see how we are being influenced.

Changing yourself because of peer pressures and social expectations is a very serious game to play. Giving in to these expectations and pressures from people considered popular can lead you down very hazardous paths. These supposedly trendy people can be highly manipulative and disregard your situation as they believe theirs is more important. Social expectations and fear of change are what maintain social hierarchies. Back in ancient times, social classes were defined by how much cattle you owned, how much land you owned, if you were of royal descent, if you had a lot of money or similar circumstances. In the modern era, people see social classes as if you are trendy, well-known or rich. People will do whatever it takes to get to the top of the social ladder. Usually, when someone obtains the necessary resources to consider themselves higher in the social hierarchy, a new trend arises, or a new product comes out. Just like that, the hierarchy dumps them for someone better. It's forever changing and can be very difficult to keep up with.

Truth be told, I am not a cool kid. I'm not in the upper levels of the social hierarchy, and I don't have the most friends on Facebook or followers on Instagram. That's because I don't really want to fit in with the in-group. Don't get me wrong; having a passion for fitting in is great and pursuing it is even better. Personally, I'm not that sort of person.

How do people fit in without submitting to peer pressure? Some people stumble upon something that sends them into the big leagues. Others try desperately to get in the most popular group in their workspace or at their school and eventually get there after making very painful sacrifices. After the blood, sweat, tears and dollars spent on making themselves match the 'in thing', there is already something else they don't have. Fitting in without submitting to peer pressure is very difficult. But understanding where you are meant to fit in is different altogether. Consider a shape toy, where certain shaped objects go in their specific place (e.g. the cube in the square-shaped hole and the ball in the circle-shaped hole). We are similar to a circle, or a star, or whatever shape you want to be (that part doesn't really matter). We try to fit into a rectangular or triangular shaped hole when we are anything but that. We try to cut ourselves off and reshape ourselves to fit in. Realistically, we never meant to fit in that place. The key is to be yourself and not let anyone change that.

Fitting in is something we have all tried to do and may continue to do in the future. These days, it may seem natural to want to change ourselves to fit in with our surroundings, or where we want our surroundings to be. If we have a new phone, we will be popular. If we embrace the latest trend, we will fit in. If we have a new car, new house or whatever is popular at the moment, we are the best we can be. Unfortunately, that isn't real. Real is having faults and moments where you think "yeah, I'm not perfect". At the end of the day, no one is. There is always room for improvement and knowing where to improve is the first step to becoming the real you, not a fake version of what you really are. People succumb to peer pressure because they want to be something they are not. I've seen many of my "good friends" try to be something that they aren't and well, to put it this way, we don't talk anymore. Many people constantly change themselves to fit in. Some people are successful in doing so, but at the end of the day, they are missing something. That something could be anything; emotions, money, relationships, happiness. How much is acceptance worth to you?

The temptation to fit in is very natural. Having something "just because" is okay, however "just because" has its limits. Being able to resist the temptation to fit in is very difficult. There is usually that expensive bag or that fancy car calling for your name. Specific temptations have different strengths. Getting help with temptations such as smoking, drinking and drug consumption has become more accessible in the past few years. That's the point I'm trying to make; temptations can become addictions. The only way for people to break an addiction is to stop. Well, that's not entirely true as there are multiple ways to break an addiction. Resisting the temptation to fit in isn't easy. People are judged, blamed and shamed if they are different. This is immensely unhealthy in society as more and more people become slaves to social expectations.

One small action can induce a great change in the world. It may not necessarily be the entire earth, but your world still matters. Take for instance the assassination of one archduke Franz Ferdinand, which resulted in millions upon millions of people dead, more injured and more still in mourning. A single action can send multiple ripples down the long run of your life. One small habit, maybe not even a habit yet, but a single unhealthy act can lead to a very dangerous lifestyle. Take alcoholics, for example. I'm not attacking anyone and am not aiming this at any person in particular. However, the impacts of an alcoholic on their family is devastating. One sip of beer, wine, or any other form of alcoholic drink can lead to one bottle, then one box, then further lead to violence, crime and even death. Making one wrong choice, one small yet insignificant choice, can dramatically alter the course of your life if you let it.

In the same way, a good habit can make everything change for the better. I remember hearing of a story of a boy who began saving up money to build a home for the homeless at the age of six. Out of every dollar he got for pocket money, he would put at least 10% of it towards a charity fund. Now he is still only a teenager, but he has raised a large sum of money for charity and is planning to continue with pursuing his charity dream. Be careful of the choices you make in life

Bad habits and decisions can lead to a tough life. Making the wrong choices can be very detrimental. That is rather extreme, and some of you reading this will take it to heart; however, that can be the harsh results of someone's circumstance. Someone can have a very unhealthy addiction to something or in some cases, someone. For some people reading this, this is a reality. But for some of you, this small piece of information can be the wakeup call you need. Peer pressure can ultimately change your life.

If someone you look up to tells you to do something you know is wrong, but it will gain their acceptance, would you do it? Would you go as far as stealing something or harming someone to gain acceptance into something that is hardly important in the long run? If you are reading this, your answer should be no. Having someone to look up to is very healthy. But if you look up to the wrong person, you may end up in more trouble than you bargained for.

Habits can be difficult to break. Usually, these habits are with us through most of our lives. The small choice we make in the beginning can lead to a lifetime of habits. Life choices are challenging to make if you don't know you're making them. People change their physical appearance because a television commercial advertises something that makes the person viewing it feel more body conscious. People change the type of clothes they wear because it's trendy (even though they don't like it themselves). People change the way they behave in certain circumstances to impress someone or be a part of something. Many people make life decisions with other people's intentions in mind instead of their own. You may think "I have made this decision because I want to be a part of this group" or "I want to have the most friends" or whatever your excuse may be. The only issue is that you are letting the expectations of other people dictate your life. That isn't something you would want. Or would you?

Some people are okay with this. Some people are okay with letting the world dictate who they associate with, what they wear, how they act, what they eat, and how they exist. It is up to you to take a stand and say, "it's my life". Being strong enough to do this is hard. To slightly ease this burden, choosing the right people to be around helps.

Questioning yourself is a great way to see where you are letting other people, groups of people or society weigh you down. Re-evaluating the type of people you associate with is essential in eliminating the impact of peer pressure on your life. Understanding that people change is important when considering this.

What do you look for in friends? A good laugh, a great night out, a long-term friendship or a one-week thing that barely ever happens? You should be looking for a group of people who are encouraging, both around you and when you aren't. People who are enthusiastic about being there for you and being your friend. You want people around you who are positive to keep your spirits up, and I don't mean the bottom of the bottle up while you chug another beer. When looking for people you would want to be friends with, don't consider cynical and manipulative people. Being around better people makes you a better person, as discussed in an earlier chapter.

Positive people are distinct in any environment based on how they react to any given situation. If someone looks at the glass half full, they are positive. Someone who sees a glass half empty is negative. How positive people react and respond to a situation is all based on their own experiences and how they choose to go through life. We all have a choice as to how we react, this being either positively or negatively. Unfortunately, this amount of people reacting positively is decreasing. Negative people are toxic, as negativity is spread easily in today's society. Logically, surrounding yourself with positive people is one of the healthiest decisions you can make in life. However, be careful not to mistake positivity for denial. They may not seem similar in any way, but when you consider the person who denies they are in a bad relationship with someone, but they live in oppression, the difference is clear. The real positive people in life are rare and hard to come by, so make sure you keep an eye out for them.

Encouraging people can be the best type of people in life. They can help you achieve goals you never thought possible and cheer you on through life. On the other hand, discouraging people can be manipulative, and entice you to do something for their personal gain. You will come across both types of people in life and distinguishing the difference between them is very important. Encouraging people should be valued and cherished because as with positive people, there aren't that many out there. But also, be warned, some people will encourage you to do the wrong things. These sorts of people are more dangerous than discouragers because they will try to deceive you into doing something wrong. I encourage you to be alert when it comes to these people.

Enthusiastic people are great to be around only if they are passionate about the right things. Many of my friends can have moments where they are overly enthusiastic about something or someone and then suddenly, I see them the next day at school, and they're lazy, deflated, sad and feel like "bluh". Enthusiasm is not an easy mood to uphold all of the time. Surrounding yourself with genuinely enthusiastic people is highly beneficial. If you do have someone who is enthusiastic at least 60% to 75% of the time, you better hold on to them because they can take you places. However, you need to be careful as to where they take you because people who are enthusiastic about the wrong things can be very dangerous. If you know this, then letting them down easy is probably the best way to go. Being an enthusiastic person can also help you find people who are similar to you.

Only in the last two years have I found some of the best friends I could imagine. I'll call them Jay and Al. They may be the two most different human beings on the planet, and they both drive me crazy. But having their enthusiasm in my life has really helped me in the past year (back in 2016). You will also find people like that in your life that will leave a distinct impression on you that makes you appreciate them. So, a big shout out to you guys if you are reading this and know who you are. Finding enthusiastic people in life is important because enthusiasm is one of the best motivators.

Pressure can be hard to deal with at times. But luckily, your friends and the people around you can help you with that. Some people go through their entire life thinking that their fake friends are real. That's not to say that imaginary friends and a ball with a face on it is not real. People often get so caught up in life that they lose track of their friends and loved ones. Real friends are there to support you through life and tell you the truth no matter how bad it is or how hard it hurts. They can be a shoulder to cry on and the second family you choose to be with. Real friends are the best people in life, but finding them is a real challenge. You need to go through a lot of blood, sweat and tears to find these diamonds in the rough. It doesn't matter how many friends you have on Facebook, how many streaks you have on Snapchat, how many followers you have on Instagram or whatever other social network following you have. A lot of the time, there is only a handful of people who are your real friends. Now you may not even know it, but some people depend on you. To them, you are their real friend. 'Real friend' isn't really the proper term, only a term used to help you understand the context. Go through life and be aware of the fake and real people out there.

Change can be very frightening. It brings new experiences and new people into your life. Naturally, people are afraid of change because they don't know what to expect. They are scared because they feel they might get hurt or possibly hurt someone else. People avoid change as much as possible because it is outside the normal cycle of their life. They want to stay with the same people, the same house, the same country, whatever is the same with their lives. But change is the best thing that could happen to you. If nothing changed in life, we would never have existed. It is because we can change that we are where we are right now. Things are constantly changing, and we fail to recognise it sometimes. Changing because of peer pressure is a danger. People can think that they are becoming something that they want to be, but they are only being influenced by society's great flaw, peer pressure. When you do change, and for whatever reason you may need to or want to, do it for you and for the right reasons. Change because you want to, not because someone else wants you to. Society's greatest flaw is entirely overrated. Ignore peer pressure and bring on the change. You never know, you might find something better in the unknown.

CHAPTER 8: HALLOWEEN ALL YEAR AROUND

The amazingly funny 1994 hit film *The Mask* features an ordinary man finding a mask that transforms him into an alter ego. As the audience views his journey as the hero of the movie, he finally learns that he doesn't need the mask to be happy in the end. This film rose to success in those years because it portrayed something that people love: a wild alter ego. The classic Clark Kent even though it's just superman with glasses and regular clothes. The superheroes we know today like the Avengers and the Justice League are all examples of alter egos in some cases. The point is, people usually embrace alter egos. They love seeing the quarrel between reality and imagination, the fight between good and evil. But superheroes aren't defined by their masks. They're defined by what they do. Now some people may only be a superhero in their own lunch box but making and wearing a mask is a very dangerous game to play. Having the courage to take our mask off and show your true identity is what real superheroes are made of.

A mask is defined as a covering for all or part of the face, worn as a disguise, or to amuse or frighten others (thank you Google). This definition clearly states that it is usually used to amuse or frighten others. It can also mean to hide something. Metaphorically, masks are alter-egos that we create to conceal something from everyone around us. Masks help people hide secrets and even help people get through some tragedy in their lives. People use masks to disguise themselves because they may be afraid of what others think of them or what others might actually see. Even in the movie mentioned earlier, Jim Carrey imitates a professional saying "we all wear masks, metaphorically speaking". The idea of a mask-wearing world brings to light the immense determination for the human race to hide and keep things to themselves. At the end of the day, we need to remove our masks. One way or another, the truth comes out, and things fall apart. A mask is a powerful thing because it can be changed as much as desired. People with multiple masks have more to deal with, in a sense that they need to remember "which one to wear".

Bravery is a very common mask to wear, especially if the person wearing the mask is a coward or not usually brave. People wear masks of bravery to impress someone, to lie to themselves, and often to face something greater than them without confronting it head-on. Another common mask is that of intelligence. Not so much intelligence, but perhaps superiority. People believe that they are better than everyone else and think less of everyone around them. Although our world is run by the powerful, the rich and the popular, we really should be considered equal. At the end of the day, we are all someone's daughter or son; we are all someone's friend; we all live and breathe on earth until one day when we die and leave everything behind. People also wear masks of pride, false superiority, etcetera. In the end, all masks have the root cause of lies, deception, fear, insecurity, and even shame.

People are constantly changing their masks to accommodate for who they're with, what they're doing, or where they are. They use different lies because they believe it's the only way they can appear popular, or get through something, or any other motive. The most common reason for having a mask is because people want to impress others. The term "dress to impress" doesn't mean changing your mask just to impress a girl or guy you like. It happens to all of us. We all have our own masks for personal reasons. Very rarely do we take them off and show the real side of us. People change their masks to fit in with the crowd and seem ordinary in some cases. They will go to highly extreme lengths to hide something or themselves from whatever or whoever is around them. A strong reason why people wear masks is that they fear what will happen if they let someone into their lives. Many movies tell stories of people who are cold and shut everyone else out because they have been "burned before" and don't want to feel that pain again. It can be very difficult to get to know those types of people and often they are the ones who need the most help.

Attention is something that many and sometimes the majority of people want. People want to be loved, to be noticed, to be thought about and spoken about all the time. People loathe other people who have the attention that they crave. Naturally, it is out of human instinct that we do our best to impress people. Most of the time, we try to impress people who don't care about us, so we can think that we have their approval. In the end, it won't change a thing. We try to impress people to fit in and be cool, or sometimes it's for standing out because we want to be noticed as something different from the rest. Often the attention is given to the masks that we wear instead of who we really are. The classic movie of a boy wanting to impress a girl, so he goes out and gets new clothes, a new hairstyle, starts hanging around different people, then suddenly BAM! He gets the girl, and they live happily ever after, right?

WRONG! Very wrong, indeed. If that were the case for everyone, it wouldn't be a very good world we live in because that's not realistic. People slip up with their masks. They come crashing down and then the dream girl slips right through his fingers. The point is, people can go to vast extremes to impress people.

Approval is not a basic human necessity or a human need, but people do love being approved of. Often, we will change ourselves and act differently when we are in certain environments. Take the schoolgirl who acts differently when she is with her friends, different when she is with her parents, different when she is with her teachers, and different when she is alone. And guys as well (just wanting to clarify that). Often people will react differently when they're around different people because they want to feel accepted. They want to feel superior or feared in some instances. People change their masks based on who they are with. If any of you have lost a very close friend, then you may understand what I am trying to convey. When I began high school, I found many new people who had become my friends. When one of my best friends had started to associate with a group of people I didn't prefer, it minorly bugged me. Next thing I knew, we had lost contact. Now that it's been about four years since then, we talk here and there but very rarely. The point is, people will change and add a new mask to their collection whenever they feel the need to.

Do you wear your mask only to impress people? Many people create them for no reason. You may even surprise yourself with the one you are wearing. People often have masks to hide their identity (or at least part of their identity). They only want to express the best parts of themselves or specific parts of themselves for them to get recognition of some sort. People have masks because they may be insecure about something. They may feel that the entire world is against them, so they put up a mask that says, "nothing can hurt me, and nothing ever will". Some people wear masks to fool themselves into thinking that their mask is their reality when it really isn't.

Are you wearing a mask? If you answered no, then you're lying. A mask of denial is what you wear. Everyone has their own masks. Well, unless you can tell any specific person anything that they ask of you, no matter what, and not lie about it. The point is, people need to understand that they are wearing a mask. The first step into getting it off is recognising it is there in the first place. Some people have a lot of trouble taking off their mask, only to find that it shouldn't be hard to take off and that it shouldn't have been on, to begin with.

Pain is the worst feeling of all. It can be the physical pain of a migraine after listening to someone talk too much. It can be mental pain like seeing something that was not meant for you that you can never un-see. Emotional pain is sometimes the worst of all pains. You could be heartbroken from a breakup or just overwhelmed with everything. People use masks to conceal their pain and suffering. And because we all have masks, we all have things to hide. What are you hiding? What do you have buried deep down in your heart that you lie about to fool the world? Is it fear? It's entirely natural to deny fear in front of your friends or family. People hide fear all the time because it can be scary. And yes, that was terrible terminology, but fear is very painful as well. Are you hiding the truth from someone because it could hurt you, them or the people around them? Often people do this in "little white lies" when in reality, the lies are there in the first place and already make up your mask. You need to be aware of why you are wearing your mask.

Dangers do come if you take off your mask. All the people your mask has fooled could be either let down or enraged when you take your mask off. Who are you trying to fool? Is it other people? The people in your office, or work, or school are the most common people that you are trying to fool with your masks. People try to fool themselves as well because accepting the truth is very painful in itself. People who deny the truth are only delaying the eventual pain if any. One day, your mask will come down, and you will realise that fooling yourself is not an easy thing to do when you know you are doing it. If you do decide to take off your mask, please don't put it back on. People are fooled by your mask and will easily accept the fact that your mask is the real you. This is especially true when you meet new people. People wear masks to protect themselves and lie to themselves. They do it to fool other people around them and in the process, diminish their relationship with the other person. But not everyone is fooled by your masquerade.

Swapping masks can be hard to do. It can be hard to juggle between multiple ones. You forget that you should be wearing the "mum and dad mask" when you are wearing the "school mask".

The point is that your masks don't fool everyone. The people who aren't fooled by your masks know you the best of all. They are most likely to be your family and your "super-duper-entirely-basically-like-family" friends. Now, these friends are hard to come by. Sometimes best-friends know the real you and not your masks. When you are around people who aren't fooled by your masks, you immediately panic and search through your bag of tricks to find something that will satisfy the needs of the people you are talking to or the environment you are in. I once heard a story about a man who visited his family for the Christmas holidays and didn't expect what he saw when he came home. It was as if nothing had changed with his family. But he was now a big-time, hotshot, business CEO. And when he forgot which mask to wear, he ended up taking it off, because his family was his family, and they were not fooled by his trickery.

Confrontation is a major mask breaker. When people are confronted with the truth, their mask breaks and crumbles apart. Often, I see interrogation scenes on CSI, or NCIS, or some other crime show on TV where the killer is confronted with the body of the victim, and they crumble. After the killer has confessed (usually it's the husband or wife, or neighbour, or jealous friend), they typically break down after being interrogated with the truth. Another reason masks break is pressure. The pressure of holding the mask up to conceal something can be hard to do when you have so many to hold up. When people's masks do brake, and their true motives are revealed, they break down and shatter like glass as I'd imagine. Most of the time, I picture that masks are like glass or that the masks we create and wear make us like glass. In the movie *Dark Shadows*, towards the end (also I apologise for the spoilers) the main character played by Johnny Depp grabs the witch. She begins to crack like she is some china doll. This is what I usually picture when our masks break and shatter before our very eyes. The causes of breaking masks greatly outnumber the reasons to create them. For the people who do lose their alter egos, the impacts can be devastating.

Fear is a great motivator in some cases. I saw a video one time where a man was trying to get in shape by doing pull-ups. To help him out, his friend grabbed a taser and held it under him for motivation. Let me address something in this video. One, it was hilarious. Two, that friend would be a pain in the ass (pun not intended as to where the taser was being held) and three, fear is a great motivator. Often people are motivated by fear because it shows what can hurt them or the people they care about. Now a taser is pretty extreme, but people keep lying to others just because they fear something. You may have seen the fear-box challenge on YouTube (if not, go ahead and watch a few). The people who do this challenge typically end up screaming and squirming before they rip their hand out of the box. In reality, it was just a teddy bear. Besides being highly entertaining, the challenge is an excellent example of how people will think something is bad when it really isn't. The fact that people stay in their bed of lies and don't risk exposure to the truth is quite natural, in a way that people always want to be right. Saving the lies is like trying to glue the mask back together to fool the same person or people. And madness is truly doing the same thing over and over again but expecting different results.

It's important to know that there are people you can open up to. Just because you have a mask and you use it to entertain certain people doesn't mean that it must always be that way. You can open up to people who know the real you. They aren't in your life because of your mask. They're in your life because of you. They know you and not the mask on a primary basis. They may also know of the masks you wear, but that's a whole other story. Sometimes it's hard to know who knows you well. Sometimes just dropping your mask and being yourself helps. But in other times, the people you have fooled may believe that the real you is the mask and want the fake you back. You need to be real with everyone. In the end, you will find the right people. When I began high school, by the end of the first year, I was completely confused with some of the "friends" I had made. By the start of my second year, I didn't like being with the people I had associated myself with. I fooled them with a mask I didn't even know I created. By the middle of the second year, I said I had enough of it, and I dropped the mask. I'd like to think that I smashed the mask with a bolt of lightning, and it was super epic with Michael Bay explosions everywhere, but I just got rid of it. It doesn't bother me anymore. I followed the words of a person who has inspired the world, time and time again.

"Be who you are and say what you feel, because those who mind don't matter, and those who matter don't mind". – Dr Seuss

True living isn't about having the biggest house, the nicest car, the best-looking spouse, the most money and whatever you think is the best thing about material life. True living is being yourself. Being yourself is the best part of life. I was once told that everyone has a purpose on this earth. By the end of their life, their job on earth is done. Truly living and being yourself is about finding where you fit in the puzzle of the world. No matter who you are, you do matter. I saw a cat poster once that said, "Be yourself, everyone else is taken". This is 100% true because no one else on this planet is exactly like you. What you have been through and what you have done in life makes you stand out from the ordinary Joe on the corner (no offence Joe). Being yourself is the most important thing to do in life. If you weren't yourself, then who would you be? Why would you want to live someone else's life and have all of their worries? The point is, being yourself is the only thing you should do in life. One of the YouTube content creators I watch is Aaron Burriss (AKA Lazyron Studios) who used to say at the end of his videos to "be true and be you". Now I've never met him before but hearing that really made me feel grateful that other people in the world want everyone to be themselves.

Genuine people are hard to find, but they were always somewhere in your life. They are usually distinct in a way that they live their lives completely different from you and everyone around them. Oh, wait, that's right. They're just being themselves. Life is better without masks. Having lies and tricking other people into thinking you're something you're not is one of the worst and most stressful things to do in life. Taking off your mask may be hard to do at first. But once it's off, you can breathe freely. You aren't constricted by anything and people can see the real, true, genuine you. If someone can't accept that you're quirky and that you do something that they don't, then they aren't the people to be around in life. There will always be people in life that just don't like you, or you just don't like. Either way, having no masks in your life is how to live life the best way possible. Now that's not to say that Halloween is sinful and evil and all that. Halloween is a time where you can play pretend and be silly and have fun. But Halloween doesn't last all year round. So, don't wear masks all through the year. Halloween is enough time for that.

CHAPTER 9: WHY AM I STUCK WITH THEM?

Everyone has a day when they're tired of all the annoying people in life. We've all had one of those days before, and for some people, that's every day. There always have been and always will be annoying people in our lives that seem to make it tougher for us. At school, in the office, at work, on the road, everywhere. But why? Why are there difficult people in our lives? This is a question frequently asked of myself because, at school, there are lots of people who annoy me. Now for privacy reasons I can't mention names of anyone and in this chapter, I won't give any examples that pertain to specific people. But sometimes there are days where the pushing and prodding, constant whining and blabbing, gossiping and teasing gets too much, and we lose our temper. Throughout this chapter, we will be exploring the "dos and don'ts" of why annoying people exist in our lives. Instead of letting them push us down, I'm going to show you how they can lift you up instead.

Jokes are intended to make people laugh. It is said that laughter is the best medicine. But if your laughing for no reason, you probably need medicine. The point is: some people tell jokes to gain attention. Attention seekers can be quite annoying. The people that will do anything to gain attention, whether through jokes or rudeness or bad behaviour, will always get the attention they want. Annoying people often want attention or aren't concerned about others around them. Eventually, these people develop habits to which they live by; habits which irritate others around them. Going through life, you will encounter highly annoying people. At times it may be who they are that is annoying, and other times it will be because of what they do. It may even be a combination of both. Most of the time, people choose to annoy others as they desire attention. Some people can't help but be generally irritable and annoying. And you never know, you might be that type of person for somebody else as well.

Positivity is a difficult attitude to keep up all the time. You will never meet a sane person that is positive 24-7 because we have our little slip-ups here and there. However, there is no real excuse for being negative all the time either. I say "sane person" because if someone is positive and happy 24-7, they must be either insane or lying to themselves as we discovered in the previous chapter. In situations where you are with annoying people, how do you view them? Do you view it as another day on the job or another ordinary day at school? How else do you view situations with irritating people? Are you frustrated with what they do, ready to lose your temper at any minute? When you are in a situation with someone who is being difficult, think of it as God giving you an opportunity to grow and learn. Now that may sound super tacky and cheesy, but we need to view every situation in a state of mind where we are patient, calm, positive and have complete control of ourselves. If we don't, who knows what will take over.

Viewing the situation from the other person's perspective can significantly assist in helping you understand how you feel about the situation. To do that, you need to observe their history. Do they do this usually? Do they want attention for a reason? If so, why do they want the attention? Asking yourself questions like this and responding to them in a logical state of mind can assist in understanding what the situation really is. You may want it to be a certain way, but in the end, it is what it is. Everyone has different perspectives, right? If I look around me at the earth that I am currently on (and hopefully you're here too), I would see houses, trees, streets, cars, people, animals and plants. If I was an astronaut and I looked out to the earth, I would see oceans, land, clouds and stars in the background. This only proves that people have different thoughts on things based on their opinion of whatever is being observed or looked at. Sometimes it might be difficult to see the situation from the other person's perspective. I once had a classmate at school that was so overly irritating that I just couldn't understand him. He did things that I couldn't reason with and understand why. It took me months upon months to understand why he was doing whatever pig-headed extravaganza he was showing. But although it took me a while, I finally understood what he was going through. Yes, it did require some background research and paying attention here and there, but in the end, I finally understood him and what his motives were. He left a little bit after I "had an awakening", but from then on, I realised that I needed a lot more patience – a whole lot more.

Pausing is a great way to catch something, whether it be waiting for a fish to bite, a sibling waiting to be caught in the act, or catching for your breath after a morning jog. Sometimes we need to stop and pause, and just breathe. And you may be thinking, "Scott, what on earth are you talking about. You just started on one topic and now you switched what you were talking about". Well, no, not exactly. When we lose our temper, we can do things that cannot be taken back. Anything that is done isn't usually taken back unless it's the wrong size, but that's not the point I'm trying to make. Taking a step back from the situation and looking at it from a different perspective can dramatically improve your temperament. That is to say that people with bad tempers need to listen up and read carefully. How do I keep my temper? It depends on what you do when you lose it. I'm not going to make a sarcastic joke like put up fliers or call the missing temperament department or whatever. You need to know what you do first in order to change it. But regardless of what you do, just stop. Take a breath. Count to ten. Make sure you're not blowing things out of perspective. Think logically about the situation that you're getting angry about. Think about what you are about to do. And finally, react accordingly.

Controlling your temper isn't always an easy thing to do. Sometimes you just lose it on the spot, sometimes its escalated from a minor twitch to a full-on spasm of anger. When there are annoying people in your life, how do you react? I've just told you what to do to calm yourself down and put the circumstance into perspective, more so a non-biased one. When you do react to the situation, look out for two things: your actions and your voice. Actions sometimes speak louder than words, but that depends on how loud those words are and what those words are. That's not the real point I was trying to make, but knowing how to react might just be the thing that helps you. Reacting appropriately involves body language, tone of voice, and what is actually being said. The body language means not going into it with your chest pumped out, fists clenched, arms crossed. It's having posture and being more assertive than aggressive. Your voice needs to be calm. When you react, make sure your tone is soft and not sharp, think about the overall situation, be positive and be careful what you say because you can't take it back.

Reacting the right way towards annoying people and annoying circumstances is the best way to benefit from these kinds of annoying people. Sometimes you lose your temper. Words are said, punches are thrown, arms are bruised, and friends are blocked on Facebook. But think about that for a slight moment before you react. It may be the difference between 543 friends and 542 friends. Sometimes God puts annoying people in our lives to test our faith and our limits. Realising that life isn't going to be easy, it's not going to be all sunshine, rainbows and unicorns can be annoying. But it is in those times that we grow as people and sometimes if there are other people with you, annoying situations shows how you can both grow in the relationship. I get that sometimes it's difficult to stay strong and keep your temper because the pressures of life can become too big, and you feel like you're carrying your entire world. If you still feel that way, stop cheating and go back and read the chapter on it! The point is, you can benefit from people who will annoy you. Being aware of these people is a great way to sort out where the opportunity is. And you never know, you might be the one to confront this person and change them forever. But do keep in mind you can't just go around changing people, when sometimes, you're the one that needs to change.

Wrong choices in life can impact not only you but the people you call friends, family and loved ones. So naturally, losing your temper in any situation is a bad thing. Sometimes you slip up and say things that you weren't meant to say and then create another mask to try and patch it up. That is almost as bad as putting a Band-Aid on a shattered window. Most of the time, people let their emotions take hold of their actions, and they forfeit their control. They make irrational decisions that don't make them better off at the end of the day. When people snap, it can happen in a split second. You make the wrong choice, and it hurts someone or something you hold dear. I've seen so many cases where people have made bad decisions when they have lost control of their anger. I recall one of my friends playing a game on his phone just about to reach his high score of 14 when BAM, he failed at 13. He was so angry that he smashed the phone out of his own hand and shattered the screen. And seriously, over a game?! Some things aren't worth the trouble. Having a good perspective of the situation you are in just before you are about to lose your temper can mean the difference between victory and defeat, between level one and level two, and in rare cases, life and death.

Issues or more so bigger issues arise when we get angry for no reason. Sometimes when we do, we make up excuses not only for other people but for ourselves to justify our temper loss. Even in my time, I've heard many excuses as to why people get all angry and worked up. They range for the immature "they started it" or "he said this to me first" to the more "in-depth" excuses that are essentially long stories that tell everyone how miserable your life is, and that the world owes you everything. The more excuses you make, the worse your life will become. Especially if those excuses are just lies used to cover up why you are really getting angry and frustrated and losing your temper. Sometimes you say, "enough is enough" and "this is too much for me to handle". Most of the time, it is more so a state of mind. People limit themselves to specific things saying, "I can't do this" and "I can't do that", but in reality, they can do those things if they put their mind to it. Now there are some logical limitations like gravity, reality, science and maths, but it depends on you. Sometimes the excuses we use to cover up our temper tantrums are the reasons why we lose it. Sometimes it isn't an excuse. But nevertheless, there is no real excuse for losing your temper when you know you can control it.

Who should change in these instances? When you are annoyed by someone who won't leave you alone or constantly pushes your buttons, who should change? Is it them? Is it your boss, your teacher, your friend, the salesman across the street, the king of Spain, the person who gets you coffee? Who needs to change? Most of the time, you'll find that it's you all along. Sometimes you need to change. We all go around naming, blaming and shaming people because they are wrong, because they didn't do this, because they can't do that. Before you start judging other people, take one good look in the mirror because you might be surprised as to what you see. Now yes, we all have gold within us and things that set us apart for how good we are. It could be your ability to sing, your intelligence, your love of art and craft, your hair, your family, your accent, anything. But look deeper. Look past the good stuff because it's not all sunshine and rainbows. We all have something to hide as I explained in the previous chapter. In the end, we need to face those demons we have. Before you start pointing fingers, look at how you are involved with this situation where you feel uncomfortable. Ask yourself, "how do I measure up?".

Challenging experiences can be dangerous and very scary. But sometimes, these experiences are what gets us into our flow in life, and they push us into our destiny. I'm now going to get you to do something for me. It won't cost anything, just read and follow along. Pick someone in your life at the moment that you are annoyed with. It could be your boss, your significant other, your friend, your family member, anyone. Now picture life without them. It may seem amazing and great and everything, but think deeper about it. Something will be missing in your life. It may take you a while to find what's missing, but once you do, you will find that they have made you a better person in some way. You need to be persistent with this because if you can't find it, you're not looking hard enough. Look at how that person has impacted you, whether it be physically, mentally, emotionally, spiritually. Really think about it. It may be as small as a laugh once, or as big as a position at work that they declined. You see, anyone that you know and that you see makes an impact on you. Eventually, it will alter you in some form or manner through the ripple effect. Have you seen the movie *Back to the Future*? Anyone of the three films? Well if you haven't, watch that movie as soon as you finish this book because it's definitely one of the classics. This series goes to prove how one change in the past can dramatically impact the outcome of the future. We may not have proper hoverboards and flying cars, but that could all be in the future. We all know nothing rational is impossible if we put 100% of our mind to it.

Learning from annoying people is a strange concept that needs some explaining. In saying that you need to learn from them, I'm not saying to learn how to be annoying. I'm saying that you need to learn from how they impact you to make you a better you. As metal sharpens metal, so does man sharpen man. That quote from Proverbs 27:17 rightly says that we need to help other people improve as other people improve us. That's not to say that you annoy everyone because "it's the right thing to do". I'm saying that you can be a better person and help someone become better in a more positive way. People learn from experience and from other people. A lot of the time, they don't listen to others and end up learning the lesson the hard way. Reacting in the right way when it comes to annoying people in your life is what really counts. Not so much how they annoy you and get under your skin, but how you react to their actions greatly impacts your future and your outcome in life. It is said that a flap of a butterfly's wing on one side of the world can create a tornado on the other side of the world. That theory just proves how we need to choose to react the right way when it comes to difficult people in life.

Approaching a situation that may be difficult is a brave thing to do in the first place. When put under the pressure of the moment, have the best outcome in mind. That is to say, when you make decisions, keep in mind that you want to be the better person in the situation. It's all about how you react, your body language, as well as your verbal response.

Regarding the verbal side of things, a study recently conducted says that people pay more attention to how people say something than what they actually say in the moment. Your friend could be going off his face in a kind, calm and collected manner and you would need to take a second look or more so, ask if he could repeat it because it would surprise you, right? If you speak to someone in a grumpy tone, no matter what you say, they will pick up on it. Because you now know and understand this, begin to apply it. If you enter a circumstance and you find it a challenge to react, pay attention to your tone of voice. Not only the volume but the tone. Are you monotone or do you have multiple tones to switch between? Are the expressions on your face saying, "I don't want to be here" or "I care enough to be here"? You can ask yourself these sorts of questions before you react. Being assertive is a lot different from being aggressive.

Aggression is the readiness or more so likelihood of someone attacking and being violent. On the other hand, assertion means showing a confident personality. That's the main difference between the terms: assertion and aggression. People get these reactions or ways to react confused and often result in going to aggression when they are threatened or want something. Usually, if you're in a bad mood, you will show more aggression than assertion. Naturally, when you growl at someone and bite back, they think you're in a bad mood or a specific mood. How do we use assertion instead of aggression? For one thing, having a scrunched-up face and crossed arms doesn't help. You need to be open chested, confident with your head held high. Show posture.

Another thing you could do to show assertive behaviour is your voice. Don't shout and yell at someone. Instead, saying something to someone with just enough force can show assertion. Make sure to stay calm, be positive, listen carefully and be open to the outcomes that you are given. Be assertive instead of aggressive in any situation and make sure to practice assertive behaviour regularly.

Appealing to the other person's motives or intentions can be a very positive decision to make when involved in a confrontation. In the last chapter, you read about not wearing a mask. So when you do go up to someone to be assertive and resolve something, go as yourself, not your mask. Making a positive decision will ultimately impact the entire area around you. That's not to say that there will be a crater around where you spoke to the person, but more so the people around you may be having the same issue. Resolving things with annoying people can be difficult to do, and it won't happen in an instant. But understanding them helps in passing the time until they do snap out of their stupidity and stop annoying you. That's a bit overboard, so let me regain my perspective while I'm at it. Having annoying people in life can be a great help to you because understanding them expands the knowledge bank in your head called your brain. When you pick up some sort of annoyance wherever you might be, the classroom, the worksite, your office, the road, a restaurant, look at it as an opportunity to grow. Not so much "why am I stuck with them" but sometimes "I'm glad to be stuck with them". And you know why? Because they might think the exact same thing about you. You never know. Keep an open mind and let the irritate become your elevate.

Take It From A Teenager

CHAPTER 10: LIPS ON A LEASH

Stop!

Where are you right now?

Who are you with?

What does it smell like?

How are you feeling?

Think back to a time where you said something you regret. It could be to an ex-spouse, an ex-best friend, a family member (because you can't have an ex-family member) and think about what that moment was like. Different right? That's the thing about thinking before you speak, people don't do it very often in the heat of the moment. Most people have no filter between their brain and their mouth. They just let their thoughts come out of their mouths and into the world around them. Words are one of the most powerful weapons in the world. Having control of what you are saying can significantly impact your reality and the way you "do life".

Books are marvellous things, aren't they? They can teleport you into a completely different world, whilst keeping you safe in the confines of the pages. In this way, words are compelling and have the power to create or destroy. You could compare words to fire, in that they create warmth and energy, but have the ability to turn a jungle to a pile of ash. Yes, that sounds extreme, but sometimes extremity is necessary.

Words make people. They can be the happy words on the birthday card you got last month, or the words on the cat poster that says, "hang in there". But they can also break people. Words that are used to blame, name and shame break people, often resulting in the loss of a close relationship or the end of a partnership. Words can be painfully brutal. When the doctor gives you the bad news, or the police come to your door. Words hold the power to create and destroy; not only physically, but also mentally and emotionally, and at times spiritually and financially

Once words are spoken into existence, it's impossible to take them back. Blurting out something hurtful or not thinking before you say something can never be undone. Trying to take words back is like saying sorry to a broken plate and expecting it to magically heal itself as if it was never broken in the first place. Everyone has moments in their lives where they wish they could go back and "un-say" something, or in some cases say something at all. But you can't, unfortunately. That is why words are very delicate. We get one shot at using them right, and if we don't, disaster can strike at any moment.

People all around the world gossip every day. People gossip on the phone, at the shops, on the way to work, at work, at home, at school, just about everywhere where two people have contact with each other. Telling other people secrets and private information about significant other people is considered gossip, especially when these supposed secrets aren't true. Gossip has ruined people's reputations and put other people's lives at risk because of it. Gossip is a weapon that is only used for destructive purposes. When gossip is spread, it eventually finds its way back to the subject of said gossip. Then all hell breaks loose. Most of the time, hair extensions get pulled out, cars get keyed, bad looks and daggers are exchanged, and people sometimes end relationships because of it. When people say something mean, cruel or downgrading about someone else behind their back, they not only bring down the person they are talking about but also themselves. Gossiping is the poison of words that has infected billions of people around the world.

Forgive and forget. Three words that are much easier said than done. People who hold grudges often neglect their own faults, choosing to linger on the wrongdoings of someone else rather than address their imperfections. Usually, grudge-holders live one of two lives. One is bitter and rotten, but the other is fake, hidden behind a mask. We need to be more cautious about what we say because we can't take words back. A single word is like a stone skimmed over a lake, no matter how many bounces you count, the ripples are endless and can never be taken back.

In the heat of an argument, information can often get distorted and ruined by emotion, specifically anger and frustration. Although we might acknowledge what's happening, we only realise after the argument that the damage done was worse than expected. All because we had to prove our point. It's honestly okay to be wrong. We learn and grow when we are wrong most of all, but nobody ever wants to be wrong. Often people don't take a moment to observe their surroundings before they speak, resulting in a lot of irreversible impacts. Before we speak, we must first understand the situation.

Begin by observing yourself. How are you feeling, and how is this impacting what you are about to say? How is this distorting the facts? You might not be able to see it at first, which is why you should pause and be patient with yourself.

Next, acknowledge and observe other people. How do you think they are feeling, and how are they involved in the facts of the situation? As you can't use a universal remote to stop time, you must do this fast, without any mistakes. You may want to take a deep breath to think about it for a moment or two, but not too deep of a breath that it seems like you are stalling the situation. Observing the situation from different perspectives can help you understand it better.

What we say isn't the only thing that people pick up on. Our body language, tone of voice and volume help us convey information without actually saying it. People who use a loud voice to say something often show signs of aggression based on their tone and body language. In the same way, someone's tone can be very aggressive without having a loud volume or specific body language. Someone might show aggression by invading your personal space and using a soft, low volume to speak. These three critical elements of communication have a tremendous impact on the way other people interpret what we say. It also comes down to the other person's perspective. If you say to someone, "Hey, you look great today", they may perceive it as though they hadn't looked great yesterday, or any other day before that. At times, it's not what you say but how you say it.

People speak in different tones, similar to different notes in music. If you say anything at all, you can play each of the notes that your voice is sounded at. People with multiple tones (especially a mixture of lower and higher tones), can often appear exciting, full of life and "out there" if you will. At the same point, people do have their off days where they don't want to put in the effort of speaking in multiple tones, sticking to one or two at most. Speaking in different tones makes things a whole lot more engaging and livelier.

The way we speak requires a specific volume depending on the impact you want to have on the people or person you're talking to. You might want to talk at a loud volume in a big room to reach more people. Or maybe you want to speak at a soft volume in a toilet cubicle because your mother is calling you urgently to check that you are still alive and healthy. Choosing the appropriate volume to speak at in everyday life is completely dependent on your personality. People often are categorised by the volume at which they speak. For instance, we all know some people who are loud and sometimes obnoxious. They can be described as extroverts, as they are outgoing and "socially confident". However, some people are quiet and enjoy the company of themselves. These people can be classified as introverts. Many times, people will talk over the top of a conversation to get their point across, even if that point has zero relation to the conversation itself. People who are reserved in their volume of speech sometimes don't get to have a say when the important choices are decided upon. Think about your own personality. Are you a loud person who likes to be around lots of people and be the centre of attention? Or are you a soft-spoken person who enjoys being to themselves with a good book? You may be somewhere in-between the two, classifying you as an ambivert. The person you are is entirely up to you at the end of the day, but you need to choose wisely. Speaking in the wrong volume at a bad time can be detrimental to the continuation of a relationship.

Although speaking is good and talking is even better, there is another side to communication. Can you guess what it is? It's listening. People often neglect this part of their interaction with others because they want to be the speaker not the spoken to. Listening can be more important than speaking because it will help you to decide what to do next. It is a valuable skill that not many people use. Even if they do, it's only to what they choose to listen to. You could give someone an hour-long speech with jokes here and there, anecdotes all around. But when you ask them about it later, they may not have anything to say about it. Listening isn't only about hearing; it's about observing, learning and analysing what other people are saying. People can pick up the wrong ideas from what is said by others, which only distorts information even more. Listening carefully and having a good understanding of the situation is vital in being successful throughout life.

Listening isn't just a straightforward thing we do when we have "our ears open". There are several different types of hearing that we use, whether we know it or not:

- The first type is what I call "in-out listening". It's where the information goes in one ear and out the other without us correctly processing it. We often use this listening when we are distracted or thinking about something else.

- The second type is called "responsive listening" which sounds good, but it isn't. This involves taking in only the information you want to hear and formulating a response to it, forgetting the other information mentioned in the process.

- The third type of listening is called "critical listening". This is where you become the judge and critique every bit of information you hear from the other person from a negative point of view. Although you take in the information, your response to it won't be right.

- The fourth type of listening is called "simple listening". It's where you do exactly that, taking in information and processing it in very simplistic terms.

- The final form of listening is called "empathetic listening". This type of listening is rarely used these days. This listening considers other information to make more accurate judgements, such as emotion, context and body language.

These five types of listening are used very often throughout our daily lives, and it's important to understand which one to use and when.

Think back to the last time you regretted saying something. Hold that moment in your mind and think about every detail. How did you feel? How did it end? How did it begin? Try to remember everything about it. What you did just then is exactly what you need to do before you say something. Considering context is important in communicating and moving towards the best possible outcome from the interaction. To begin, you must first understand how you are feeling in the moment and the environment you are in. Thinking about your feelings in the heat of the moment can be tricky, so you may want to pause to compose your thoughts. Next, empathise with the other person to the best of your ability, and try to understand how you would react if you were in their position. Then finally, decide to say something or not. When it does come to this decision, be careful of the repercussions it might have. What you say and do today ultimately impacts the rest of your future.

Throughout human history, people have used speeches to change the world. One of the most famous speeches in all of history is the "I have a dream" speech by Martin Luther King Jr during the March on Washington. Witnessed by over 250,000 people, his speech is still recognised as one of the most influential speeches to have ever been presented. The power and passion behind the words spoken inspired a nation and the world entire. Going back much further in history, the sermon on the mount is yet another famous speech, given by Jesus of Nazareth. Found in Matthew 5-7, this speech has influenced Christianity for centuries and continues to inspire millions of Christians to this day. Words have the power to change history, whether we know it or not. Although we might never see the full impact of our words in our lifetime, the world deserves to hear what you have to say. Afterall, words are what makes or breaks our world.

At the dawn of the 21st century, it has become even easier to express ones' opinions through words with the growing popularity of social media platforms. This has made it even easier for people to make a difference, providing the ability to reach more people all around the world. Just as people express their opinion, they need to be able to listen to the opinions of others as well. At times, we may neglect the importance of speech because we listen too much. By this, I refer to a ridiculously small percentage of people in the world who listen more than they speak. Without your voice, getting your point of view and ideas into society is a whole lot harder. Some of you reading this may not be able to speak; however, when I refer to speech, I mean the expression of your ideas and opinion. Whether it be through music, or art, or dance, or writing, expressing yourself is one of the most important things to do in life.

Communication involves two core components, listening and speaking. These go hand in hand because one is inferior without the other. How can you expect to be heard when you don't speak up? How can you expect to hear something when you're not even listening? Unfortunately, a vast majority of teenagers these days (and also adults in many cases) speak more than they listen. My dad always says to me, "God gave you two ears and one mouth, which means you should listen twice as much as you speak". We need to establish more of a balance between when we speak and when we listen. Understanding when, where and how to speak can be very difficult, especially if big changes are currently taking place in your life. Being a good listener is just as good as being a good speaker.

Now that you have a somewhat better idea of the pros and cons of thinking before you speak, venture out into the world and test what you have learnt. Just make sure that you keep your lips on a leash.

CHAPTER 11: I'M NOT CRAZY, AM I?

Madness can be observed in many different forms, emitting several different symptoms. It may be a twitch, a frantic mumble, chaotic tendencies, horrible mood swings and the list goes on; but that's not the point I'm trying to get at here. Some say that the first sign of craziness is talking to yourself. You may be thinking, "well that's dumb, I always talk to myself, and I'm completely sane". And you'd be right in thinking that, because talking to yourself is not a sign of craziness.

Talking to yourself is similar to thinking. We think in our own voice and ask ourselves questions about whatever is happening in our lives. This is an involuntary aspect of human life. Without thought, we wouldn't be able to function for ourselves. Talking to yourself is a great way to seek personal advice, because the best person to understand your situation is you.

This is typically the point that you realise that you've wasted your time reading just over half this book because the author is crazy. Well, although I have not been formally tested, I am pretty sure I'm not mad. Talking to yourself is an entirely normal thing to do. In fact, I would encourage you to speak to yourself, whether it's said out loud or kept in your head. Self-talk is very helpful in boosting your self-esteem and working out personal issues or problems. However, some people might be afraid to talk to themselves in the mirror, fearing what might be said back.

CAUTION! BE WARNED! Speaking to yourself out loud will make you seem crazy to everyone around you, no matter how well they know you. This does have some sorts of limitations around it, like speaking to yourself in private. When it gets to the point that you are causing a major public disturbance, there seems to be an issue. Back to the point, speaking out loud has several pros and cons. Besides the fact that it might make you look like you've lost your marbles, speaking out loud is sometimes not necessary. Self-talk is healthy but not if spoken aloud in public or in front of people (or heaven forbid at people). Let me give you some context and frame this for you. Asking yourself the odd, "where did I put my keys?" or "I added salt, right?" is natural. It helps you recall information you are questioning. At the same time, having a full-blown conversation about your co-worker and acting out the different parts like a one-man show, completely aloud, might mean a few nuts and bolts are missing up there.

Controlling how you think might be just as crucial as self-talk. Being oblivious to the repercussions of our actions can turn us into slaves to our thoughts and emotions. When someone cuts you off in traffic, and you find yourself in front of them, you might decide to slow down a bit and go 20 in a 60 zone. By this point you're pretty happy with yourself thinking, "that's right, I showed them", only to get pulled over by the police shortly after. It might not seem like it but because you let your emotions get the better of you, it cost you a $150 fine just for something as petty as teaching someone a lesson about not cutting you off.

Our thoughts and emotions can sometimes get the better of us. Sometimes during the day, you might drift off into your own little world and become lost in your own imagination. Don't get me wrong, imagination is the very fruit of life that powers and inspires the world for the better. It only becomes an issue when you find yourself imprisoned by the red queen after drinking tea with the Mad Hatter and the Cheshire cat, all the while sitting at the steering wheel with a green light ahead of you.

Ideas are often refined with positive self-talk. Reasoning out several possible outcomes to an issue can help you understand it better, and perhaps even reach the most beneficial solution. Although people often use self-talk frequently in their day, this self-talk is rarely positive. You might see in an overdramatised movie where a girl is dumped by her first love, then it pours with rain, and she has to walk home by herself. When she gets home, she goes to cry in the bathroom and think, "what's wrong with me", or, "aren't I pretty enough". Not to say that being dumped means that you shouldn't cry and hurt, just be sure that it doesn't become a habit (the negative thoughts and self-talk that is). Even if you haven't been through a breakup, today's society portrays enough images of unachievable perfection that make us question ourselves. Negative self-talk is highly toxic and can ruin even the brightest of people. People can fall into bad habits (including negative self-talk) after emotional disturbances or traumatic events.

One of the most toxic by-products of negative self-talk is the possibility of blaming others rather than blaming yourself. Not to say that other people can't be responsible for wrongdoings, but placing unsolicited blame on others can ultimately lead to the destruction of multiple relationships. We can't precisely control what other people think, say or do. Life is full of people who will think, say or do the wrong things; some of which you won't agree with and some which hurt you. In the end, blaming is wrong; regardless of its other people or yourself.

Types of Thought

Conscious Thought

Jiminy cricket is known as the little cricket who made a home in Pinocchio's head. He is often recognised as Pinocchio's conscience or the voice of reason. In the same way, we all have a jiminy cricket in our heads. Our conscience is the voice we have in our heads that advocates for our moral sense of right and wrong. When we think, we have a voice in our head that expresses our thoughts. To put in another way, our conscience is our thoughts.

What is the first word that pops into your mind when you think of the word "summer"? It may have been sand, or sun, or hot, or ice-cream, or even winter. It can be anything in the world at all. When you thought of that word, you consciously said it in your head because you had to think about it. This voice of reason is called your conscience. You could see this conscience of yours as an angelic version of you on your right shoulder and a devilish version of you on your left shoulder. These two characters can help you reason out what to do next or how to respond to a situation only if you choose to consult them first.

Sub-Conscious Thought

Subliminal messages are often used to impact and change the subconscious thought process. "Subconscious thought" is a term I use to describe thoughts that are impacted by aspects of society. Subliminal messages are concepts and ideas that are all around us and make us feel or think of specific things. For instance, seeing a movie character eat an incredibly aesthetic-looking meal will often result in the audience feeling hunger for that same meal. In the same way, small things such as colours, shapes and even sounds can change the way we think. Tricks and illusions are used in society to impact on our subconscious thought. Society may say one thing but imply a hidden meaning underneath it. For instance, showing a perfectly toned, six-packed model with rippling muscles at the front of a fitness magazine impacts the subconscious thought and can make the person looking at it feel insecure about themselves. This can have even more flow-on effects, impacting readers physically and emotionally, forcing them to go to extreme lengths just to match the so acclaimed "perfect" image portrayed by society.

Unconscious Thought

Reflexes, habits and reactions all fall under what I call "unconscious thought". The primary functions of the body (like breathing) are maintained even when we are unconscious. However, when I refer to unconscious thought, I refer to the thought that comes naturally to us. When you are nervous before your meeting with the big boss in town, you might begin to sweat, fidget, look around, tremble, your breathing could quicken, and you could get incredibly dizzy. But what do these types of thought have to do with you?

Prophesies are usually spoken of in fairy tales and stories of old. Whether it be the ancient prophecy of the chosen one coming to unite kingdoms or the prediction of the child destined to take the kings place, stories through history have used prophecies as a means of portraying destiny.

Have you ever wondered what your destiny is or what the universe has in store for you?

Self-talk can help you determine your own prophecy if you choose to use it correctly. What we think and what we say are two vital aspects that can help define our future. Have you ever had a full cup of hot coffee in your hand and start to think, "don't spill it, don't spill it, don't spill it", over and over again; only to eventually spill it? The thing is, the universe can give you precisely what you ask for, but with a catch. You might think of the universe like a genie, just not the Aladdin kind of genie. Whenever you say negative phrases like "I hope I don't", or "I won't" or similar, the universe drops the negatives. So instead of "don't spill it", the universe hears "spill it, spill it, spill it" and gives you exactly what you want. It also boils down to a case of psyching yourself out through self-talk. However, if you learn how the universe works, why not use self-talk to your advantage?

The term 'attraction' is used when one thing is drawn to another. The way we think and what we think about is naturally attracted to us. Some recognise it as destiny, others call it fate, and some know it to be God's divine plan. God doesn't pick up on the don'ts, won'ts, and no's because anything is possible with Him. To put it simply, we are what we think and speak into being, a principle recognised as the self-manifestation principle. When you wake up in the morning and look yourself in the mirror, saying something like "hey good-looking" might make you sound full of yourself, but you aren't wrong either. Speaking praise into your life will naturally attract blessings to your life.

Some of you might know of the story of Morris E. Goodman (AKA the Miracle Man), but if you don't, let me explain. The year was 1981, and Morris E. Goodman was involved in a plane crash, leaving him fully paralysed. Unable to talk, swallow or even breathe on his own, the doctors said he would never recover from the paralysis. Although the doctors didn't know he heard them, he used positive self-talk to prove them wrong. Slowly, he began to regain control of his eyes, blinking to show that he was still with them. Little by little, he started to breathe on his own, talk, move his limbs, and before you know it, he was walking out of the hospital unassisted by anyone. By continually encouraging himself just to blink, or breathe, or speak, Morris went on to prove all the doctors wrong. Big things can come your way if you use self-talk to your advantage.

Thinking logically and retaining context is important when employing self-talk, especially when considering the self-manifestation principle. For example, although you might tell yourself every day that you're going to dig a hole through the centre of the earth all the way to China, it's unfortunately not possible. However, that doesn't mean that you don't dream big or have broad goals and aspirations. If you don't dream big, how can you hope to make the most out of life? Maintaining a logical point of view also means understanding that although some things might seem unachievable right now, the future is full of limitless possibilities.

Positive thinking can change your entire life. Altering your mindset can have significant impacts on the way you live life. Freeing yourself from the usual, grouchy, negative mindset of the past is the first step in improving your life. Changing the way you think isn't always going to happen instantly. It may take a few days, a few weeks or even a few months, because there will always be the temptation to fall back into your old way of thinking. And the truth is, life isn't all happy unicorns, sunshine and rainbows. It's okay to have a bad day every once in a while. But don't let yourself see that as the constant norm. Better things are waiting for you. You have a bright future, and God has great plans for your life. Be the person that says, "I can, and I will". Go the extra mile, do that extra kilometre on the running machine, take that extra 5 minutes to play with your dog before work (but don't let that make you late for job), make the most out of every day, every hour, every minute and every second. You've got a lot to live for, no matter where you're from, who you are and where you are going.

Changing your mood is something everyone struggles with. Isolating your emotions from the facts is even harder when your emotions are strong. A vast majority of people wake up in the morning, open their eyes and wish that they still had more time to sleep. Getting out of bed can be difficult, especially considering that your pillows have accepted you as one of their own and moving would betray their trust. But that's entirely beside the point. Verbalisation is essential to becoming what you believe because you need to hear it physically. No matter how loud and bellowing your head voice might be, you need to verbalise it. Wake up every morning and say something like, "I'm blessed and feeling my best".

Verbalising these sorts of somewhat "cheesy" affirmations can fill your morning with life. Try telling yourself, "Today will be a great day. Today is the day that I change the world". It could even be something like making an extra sale, or being on time for work, or sticking to your diet. Beginning with small goals and working your way up can be a great way of starting a positive goal-setting habit.

Many people might define a perfect life as having a two-story, luxurious, modern house on the hill, being in the perfect relationship with the perfect spouse and having the dream job (which may be no job at all might I add). This ideal life has all the best friends, all the best family and everything goes your way. Unfortunately, this image of the perfect life isn't real. You might have all these aspects of the "perfect life", but you can never achieve perfection. The perfect life, according to all leading televisions, is not an achievable life. No one is perfect. At some point in our lives, we've made mistakes. We've been greedy, or jealous, or negative, or angry. We've had too much to eat, said something we've regretted, or done something we shouldn't have. And we will continue to make mistakes in the future. But every single one of these mess-ups makes us human. The important part is making sure that when we do make mistakes, we learn from them and strive towards the best version of ourselves. Just because perfection can never be achieved, it doesn't mean we stop striving to be the best we can possibly be. There's no point in obsessing over all the material things that will be outdated sooner than you can get your hands on it. Work towards being your best physical, emotional, mental, spiritual, psychological (and all the other -al's out there) self.

So, what should you think? It's a rather odd question to ask near the end of a chapter, but really think about how and what you should be thinking. Should I be thinking positively or negatively?

Should I be thinking about big dreams or small hopes? Should I think about having another slice of cake or having a salad (which is completely obvious if you ask me)? Now it's all up to you because you are you. There is no one else like you in the world. You are the only version of you, even if you are an identical twin. You are the most unique person to be you because no one is more "you-er" than you are.

Go and live each day with the best in mind. Don't be afraid to talk to yourself in private and aloud, or in public and in your head. Be a blessing to people around you and make the most out of every opportunity. Do all you can to show glory to God and let him take you places you have never thought possible before today. Say to yourself, "I am blessed. I am favoured. I am successful. I am good-looking. I am healthy. I am strong. I am brave. I am courageous. I am here for a reason. I have a can-do attitude. I'm not crazy, am I?"

CHAPTER 12: THE DAVID WITHIN YOU

Fear. We all experience it. It could be the fear of small spaces, the fear of spiders or snakes, even the fear of death or losing someone close to you. Throughout our lives, we experience different fears that can stop us in our tracks. Naturally, we will choose between fight, flight or freeze. Making the right decision is important when we experience "David and Goliath" moments in our lives. Whether we freeze up in the moment or send the rock hurdling at his head, we all have to make careful decisions about how we face our giants. It represents the most significant challenges in our lives, ones which are completely unavoidable.

As we all know, the story of David and Goliath tells of a young boy defeating a giant in an unlikely battle for supremacy over the kingdoms. In the same way, we all have challenges in our lives that we must overcome to reach our full potential. These are different for everyone because everyone is different. But unlike David, we will face multiple Goliaths in our life as we are challenged to change.

Strength, bravery and confidence are some of the things you will need when you face your toughest challenge. As you approach the overbearing test ahead of you, don't show fear. Be strong and believe that you will come out of the battle stronger than you were before. Although some people think they need to rely on others for everything, when you face it, you must be the one who slings the stone. You, yourself, must overcome this obstacle and make it an opportunity. This opportunity could skyrocket you into your destiny and into success.

Facing your greatest obstacle won't be as simple as 1, 2, 3. You might have to take a few steps back before you can take a step forward. The story of David and Goliath teaches us that we need to take courage and stand out from the crowd. We need to believe that we have the power to defeat giants in our lives and that no matter what is said or done, we can achieve what was thought to be impossible. Whether it's a job promotion, expressing your feelings for another person, or overcoming a phobia, it's entirely and ultimately yours to conquer.

Timing is essential when confronting your Goliath. Going in too early and you will head to battle unprepared and rushed. Going too late, and you could miss the battle completely. We can rarely plan out the right timing. It may come as a surprise, throwing you in the firing line with no notice, or perhaps a slow and steady process that you need to watch for. Although the sole purpose of a monumental challenge is to bring you closer to your destiny, be warned: some goliaths aren't yours to fight. Some battles are intended as the war for someone else. You might help them onto the battlefield, but that doesn't mean you need to fight for them. When the moment is right, you'll know when you face your Goliath.

As our greatest challenge can be anyone or anything, it may even be you. Yes, that's right, it's you against you. Sometimes, you don't even know you are fighting against yourself. At times, we purposely hold ourselves back from big opportunities based on deep-rooted, personal reasons. It may be the fear of the unknown, fear of change or fear of how others think of you. When you do come up against yourself, you need to know that everything will work itself out in the end and that you are strong enough to take this on. When presented with a high-risk opportunity to succeed, we may choose not to go for it because of that risk. You miss out on the opportunity of a lifetime because you fear the unknown. This is what I mean by "you against you". Sometimes we look high and low for what is holding us back and forget to check the mirror. That is why self-talk is vital for success and defeating your Goliaths in life, whoever or whatever they may be. Be courageous enough to say, "yes, I am afraid. But I am brave enough to stride through fear with confidence".

Being brave and looking brave are two completely different things, and it can be quite difficult to be brave. You may ask someone for their opinion, but that only makes it worse. You could ask a role model what they think, and their response could confuse you. However, the one place that we can always find bravery is in God. Having faith in God is what gives people the courage to face their Goliaths. It gives them hope that although they have cancer, they are going to beat it with a smile on their face. It gives them hope that although they are petrified of heights, they are going to conquer their fear and go skydiving. It gives them hope that although they are a bit of a scaredy-cat, they are going to talk to the person they like. The Bible reassures us that everything is in God's hands and that everything will be alright in the end. Despite all the troubles you may be facing now, God can give you courage beyond lions and bears.

Getting stuck in a day-to-day schedule and routine can force you to miss your chance to step up when no-one else will. It is only because David stepped up that he made history. Everyone was far too scared to take on this 9-foot-9 giant with all his lethal weaponry and armour. Sometimes we need to break from the mediocre and take a risk, especially when no-one else wants to. Life gives us endless opportunities to do so, but we simply ignore most of them. At school, at work, on the road, at home, just about everywhere, there is an opportunity to do something right, something good that no one else is prepared to do. Being courageous enough to step out of your comfort zone is not easy, but it's also not impossible. You need to be the person you want to be, not who everyone else wants you to be. There is no use in trying to please everyone else in life, because if you do, you risk missing your David and Goliath moment, or perhaps moments.

Many strive for recognition. You might think that stepping up will be a way of making other people recognise you as someone brave, confident, daring, fearless and a true leader. When no one takes charge in a tense situation, all hell can break loose. This is typically seen in group projects. At school, the very notion of group projects creates a gravitational pull between friends. Some groups get work done, and others don't. In every group, there are usually several different types of people. The funny one, the smart one, the freeloaders, the irritators and of course, the leader. Without leadership, what would happen? Would work get done by the entire group? Not typically. People need to take charge of situations to increase efficiency and stand against the chaos of do-what-ever-you-want-ness. When the time comes, you need to take hold of the situation and face your deepest, darkest Goliaths.

Speaking words of praise and blessing to yourself is a highly effective way to begin prophesying your future. This isn't all mumbo jumbo as I've spoken about in the last chapter. Speaking words of favour in your life is the best way to attract blessings towards you. When you wake up, take about 5 minutes or so and say everything that you are grateful for (without falling back to sleep). It could be your family, your friends, your pets, your house, your car, your job, anything in the world that you are grateful for. Once you do that, say everything that you want out of today. These could be, "I want to be a more positive person today", or "I want to be more patient on my way to work", or "I want to be more confident today". You need to say and believe this with every part of your being. I know it sounds weird, but you need to be positive and enthusiastic about prophesying your future. When you have a great attitude and an optimistic outlook on life, you will attract better experiences and opportunities.

Loading your slingshot can be difficult when you're up against a Goliath. For starters, loading your slingshot involves understanding what your Goliath is. This is entirely subjective and unique for everyone. What are you loading your slingshot with? Is it a rock? No. Is it a bullet? Hopefully not. Is it a way to change Goliath's Wi-Fi password rendering him useless? Well, that could also work, but NO! It's none of those things because sometimes you can't prepare for it. Sometimes it catches you off guard at an unexpected moment. Knowing this, what do you do to prepare?

First, we need an attitude check, or as my parents like to call it, a check-up from the neck up. You need to have a positive attitude towards your obstacle. We might have some days where we aren't feeling in a good mood or just feeling out of it. However, we can't afford to stay like that forever.

Next is maturity. Have you ever been in a fight with someone and they do something funny or humorous? Having a sense of maturity and understanding is very important throughout life. Although it's good to relax and be childish sometimes, it doesn't mean we stay like that.

So, once you have a positive attitude and some degree of mental maturity, you should be ready to load your sling, take aim and FIRE!

The shot you take at Goliath might miss completely and hit the soldier with the frilly helmet at the back. That is to say, sometimes we have a swing and a miss when it comes to facing our hardships. Life is full of failures with occasional success here and there. But there is glory in failure. Every failure is an opportunity in disguise. We can learn a lot more from losing than winning. When asked about his failures to create the light bulb, Thomas Edison said:

"I have not failed; I have just found 10,000 different ways that won't work."

How is that for perspective! Although he failed such a large amount of times, he succeeded in creating the first light bulb, showing us that failure brings us closer to success. In the same way, a broken relationship might be very painful, but it's also one heart-break closer to your soulmate. There are thousands of different ways you can put it. Regardless, we shouldn't be afraid to take another shot when we miss.

"Aim for the moon. Even if you miss, you will land amongst the stars."

Understanding this and applying it is very important instead of just reading words off a page. Don't be afraid to take another shot. It means that you are one step closer to defeating your Goliath and finally hitting your target right between the eyes.

Not all of your shots will hit your target, but eventually one of them will. Each shot you take is a leap of faith. Going out and embracing the challenge means you are taking a massive leap of faith. Taking this leap poses the fear of the unknown, one of the main fears people experience in life. Fear seeps into people because of the uncertainty of the outcome and the idea that something might go wrong. People fail to see that although something might go wrong, something might go right as well. There is beauty in never knowing what could happen. You could take your shot and hit the wrong person. Or you could miss your target and hit an even bigger, better one right in the bullseye. We take many leaps of faith in our lives: taking our first steps, trying new foods, buying our own homes and cars. Everything we do requires an aspect of faith because to do something new, we need to believe that it is possible and achievable. When we do take the opportunity, we can get the biggest rewards at the end of it all. Being able to take a risk and go for your dreams is very scary, but very powerful.

When you face your Goliath, there will be people who will try and discourage you, people who tell you that you shouldn't fight or that you're dumb for thinking you can. Even David experienced this in 1 Samuel 17:28, where his brothers said to him, "Why have you come down here? And with whom did you leave those few sheep in the desert? I know how conceited you are and how wicked your heart is; you came down only to watch the battle." Even his family were telling him that he shouldn't be there, trying to put him down and discredit him. People will try to hinder you from taking on your Goliath because they may think it is the right thing to do or believe that you can't do it. A lot of the time, people will try to manipulate you for their own benefit. These people are only concerned with what they will get out of your battle, whether you win or not. Being aware of these types of people is important because they aren't healthy for your life. That's not to say that you have no one around you and be a scrooge in life, it is to say that you need to be careful when you are heading off for battle. You need to make the right decision and choose your weapon carefully to suit whatever Goliath you may be facing.

Where else can you find courage and bravery? At times, it may not be a question of courage and bravery. Some of the great feats in history were achieved not through heroics but through the sheer determination to survive. Finding motivation can be easier than you think. Recognising the reward after defeating your Goliath can be a great motivator when needed. If you have an incentive at the end of a long journey, you will be more determined to complete the journey and make it to the end. However, bravery doesn't always bring results. There is a very thin line between bravery and stupidity. It takes a very keen eye to see the difference between them.

Furthermore, just because you are brave doesn't mean what you are doing is right. You need to understand your Goliath and face it with bravery but make sure you are slinging your rock towards the real enemy and not the side distraction. Find bravery in the people around you. Your friends, family, co-workers, role models and even your pets. Face your Goliath with a smile on your face and bravery in your heart.

Fights are fought on the great battlefields of the world with guns, armour, tanks and other instruments of warfare. They are also fought in the arenas and cages for entertainment. But the internal fights we fight daily are rarely recognised. Sometimes the worst battles of the world are fought in the hearts and minds of everyday people. Deciding between two options, each of which hurts someone else, is a tough decision to make. In saying this, internal battles can drive us to be better people. As the saying goes, it's not the size of the man in the fight but the size of the fight in the man, or woman, that counts. We all go through battles within ourselves that make us better people in the long run. This is important in facing your Goliath because we will all come face to face with a major opportunity that needs to be tackled. Instead of obstacle or enemy or problem, I said opportunity. That's because there are always opportunities in everything, whether it's in the good or the bad. We need to be able to embrace these times as opportunities. We need to have that drive for success and use all of our strength, faith and passion to make the best of our battles.

Knowledge is power if used in the right way, and there is a lot of strength in knowing the right things. It doesn't matter how big we are or how we physically appear. Between David and Goliath, there was a 4-foot difference in height. Although David was tiny, he was mighty. That is all because of what was inside of him. The passion, the motivation, and the grace of God led David to defeat Goliath. You shouldn't be worried about dressing to impress, eating only healthy foods, being friends with "cool" people or any of that because you are more powerful than you know. You have the potential to defeat giants with mere stones and become kings or queens in your own walk of life. It may not mean that you get to rule the kingdom and live in a fancy castle, but seeing yourself as a king or queen in your own eyes is important. Once you defeat your Goliath, you will see yourself as a completely new, different, and better person. Go out today and live your best life. But always be ready to face your Giant, no matter what it is. And when you do face your Goliath, make sure to embrace the David within you.

CHAPTER 13: HOW TO SPELL RESPECT

Throughout our lives, we see many forms of respect. Whether it be low respect, high respect or no respect at all, we treat people with specific degrees of respect based on our relationship with them. The word itself means to hold in esteem or honour. Respect is a scarce quality to come by in people these days, especially in a social atmosphere. Typically, in the 21st century, we often neglect the need and perhaps want for respect as it does not pose any gain. We often adopt a mindset that says, "if I don't get respect, you don't either". In this way, respect is thrown right out the window, and no one bothers to ask why. Through the next chapter, I will be discussing with you the role respect plays in our world and how it can make a greater impact.

How is respect spelt? You may think of the iconic song from 1965 called "Respect" by Otis Redding, made famous in 1967 by Aretha Franklin. As the song goes, "R, E, S, P, E, C, T, find out what it means to me". In the following chapter, we'll be doing just that. We are going to find out what the real meaning of respect is.

R: Recognising who you respect and why

Respect involves recognizing other people for their achievements and their goals. When you have respect for someone, you may not even know them personally. For instance, for all the people who have fought in a war, whether it be in World War 1, World War 2 or the recent wars in the middle east, I have great respect for them. They put their lives on the line to protect their countries. I have great respect for the police department because of their position in society and how they uphold the law. I have great respect for the doctors, nurses and scientists who are healing people and restoring lives the best they can. I have great respect for the firemen and people in the fire department who are at the public's aid in dire emergencies. These are just some of the more common places to show respect in the world. But respect is rarely shown to teachers, people who serve you at the counter, to shop owners and so on. These people play a significant role in society but don't even recognise it themselves. I encourage you to write a list of all the people in your life that you respect. Why do you respect them, and how have they impacted your life? Recognising this is the first step to understanding what respect means.

E: Earning respect

Earning respect is a two-way street. You can't expect people to respect you without showing them respect as well. Gaining respect from people can be achieved in several different ways, but showing respect is not hard at all. And yet, no matter how easy it is to respect someone, there will always be people in your life that don't show respect to anyone but themselves. They think they are better than everyone else and deserve everyone's respect without needing to show it back. Earning respect is a two-way street because where respect is shown, respect is returned. It may not be an instant "BAM! I respect you". It may take a bit of time, but being respectful never hurt anyone. Showing respect is much easier than trying to force people to show it to you.

S: Showing gratitude and respect

People's achievements and services, either for you or others, can earn them respect based on what they do and how they do it. We can respect people because they can complete tasks that we can't do by ourselves. Showing gratitude to other people is important when expressing genuine respect. Respect shown out of sarcasm is a very dull, fake and meaningless type of respect that will end up hurting either the person receiving it or the person giving it. It is obvious when someone is giving you their genuine respect. Some people live their entire lives based on the idea of obtaining and getting the respect of someone they admire and hold in high regard because they are important. So naturally, showing respect to others involves some depth of gratitude.

P: Process of gaining respect

Action isn't the first step in the process of gaining respect as most people would be led to believe. The first step to gaining respect is about attitude. Having the right frame of mind is vital to gaining respect. The wrong frame of mind can have a devastating impact on the style and type of respect that is achieved. Rulers in the past have gained their respect because of their position on the social ladder. The respect shown to most rulers in the past was out of fear. The other side of respect is gained from doing good, or more so doing the right thing. The second step in the process is communication, not only with yourself (about why you want respect) but with other people as well (questioning whether they respect you and why or why not). The final step in getting respect is action. After having the right attitude and understanding where you can improve, you can make the necessary changes so that you can obtain the proper respect in the right way.

E: Empowering others through respect

Empowering others is the fifth aspect of finding how respect works in your life. Respect is all about empowering others. It's about making them feel like what they have achieved was worth it and that it didn't go unnoticed. Even if it is as small as saying thank you, showing respect naturally empowers people. It makes them feel that they are more than what they think they are, and this can be significantly beneficial to one's mental health and attitude. When a parent tells their teenage child that they can go out in the city by themselves for the first time and that they trust them, the teenager usually feels as though they are respected because they have trust. They feel as though they are more than what they are because they have the trust of their parents, and having that trust is very important as it is easy to break. Respect is about empowering other people because when we show respect, we let other people know that we are there for them and that we see them. When people receive respect, they are satisfied with what they have become or more so who they have become.

C: Consistency of respect

Consistent respect is one of the hardest things to keep. Respect is very similar to trust in that it is very delicate. People choose to give others respect. However, they can easily take it away. When your friend does something for you, you have respect for them because of what they have done. But as soon as you find out they have done something wrong, something that could potentially negatively impact you, you start to lose respect for them. It may happen in an instant, or it may happen over time. But when respect is lost, it can be challenging to get it back. Typically, people tend to only remember the negatives of a person's past instead of the positives. Respect is hard to come by as more and more people look to the negatives of a person before they decide if they respect them or not. Usually, people interpret the first pieces of information they are given and give respect accordingly. My dad was in the car one day, and he saw an open van. On the side of the van, it said the word laughter. Naturally, this implies that the company is all about bringing happiness to people's lives and making them laugh. It was just at this time that the worker closed the door to reveal the letter "s" in front of the word laughter, turning the word into slaughter. At this point, people would lose respect because of what the word slaughter implies. As such, we need to be careful about respect and how consistent we are when we show it.

T: Treating others right

Acknowledging other people for what they have done is a simple type of respect. When we want to obtain respect, we should follow the golden rule: treat others the way you would want to be treated. That doesn't mean buying a Lamborghini for a stranger. By "treat people the way you would want to be treated", I mean casually. If you are nice to other people, genuinely nice and not fake nice just to get something, they are more inclined to be kind to you. Moreover, how we respect others reflects on how we respect ourselves. Unfortunately, self-respect is somewhat hard to see in modern society. People who do reckless, careless things, who damage their bodies in every manner or form, don't show respect to themselves. To understand what respect means to you, you need to be able to treat others the way you want to be treated so that you respect others the way you would respect yourself.

Respect is gained in several ways as I've said before. There are two main types. The first type is fear. Respect gained out of fear is usually shallow and dull. It's not easily expressed, and when you have respect from someone out of fear, it usually leads to demise for either party. The other type of respect is achievement-based. When people achieve goals, go out to be the best they can be and change the world in the most dynamic way possible, people respect them. That's not to say that you give a million dollars to your neighbours. What we do every day can gain us respect from our loved ones, our co-workers, our friends, and even just the people around us that we may not even know. You may have no idea who someone is, where they come from, what their goals and aspirations are in life but still have immense respect for them because of what they have achieved. Their achievements may not even benefit the world. It may be a personal achievement. It may be living through and beating cancer, or it may be building their dream home or losing weight. Whatever it is, people achieve great things in their lives, and those who are fortunate enough to see it are the ones who show the most respect to these people.

You must show respect to yourself. If you don't have respect for yourself, how can you expect to go all the places you want to go, see all the things you want to see and do all the things you want to do in life. Showing respect to others can seem more important than showing respect to yourself. However, having self-respect is also essential, considering how unique and special you are. Being able to show respect to yourself can be hard, especially in today's times. People fall into stereotypes and begin to lose respect for themselves. They try to fit into the mould of the nerd, or the popular girl, or the desk worker, or so on. It's not other people's world you should be holding up, yours is already heavy enough as it is. Showing respect to yourself can mean a lot of different things to a lot of different people. It could mean taking some "me" time every fortnight instead of at the end of every year. It could mean spending more time with your family instead of at work. It could mean not getting a tattoo of lips eating a chicken wing on your bicep so every time you flex, it chews. Having self-respect is very important throughout your life.

Cultures and ethnicities are different around the world. The cultural practices in China are very different from the cultural practices in America. That's because people are all different in the world and have their own beliefs. This is why it is essential to respect other people. The golden rule is treating others the way you want to be treated. So why would you want to be stereotyped because of the food you like and your background? Why would you want to be ridiculed because of what a very small population in your culture has done? People who condemn others because of their culture have it all wrong. Just because one person or some people are like that, doesn't mean all people in that culture are. We need to understand that all people are different and that we all come from different places in the world, growing up with different values and becoming different people. It's only right that we treat others with respect. Without respect, all that's left is destruction and chaos. It may not be apparent at first, but a wedge between people can lead to more significant impacts over time. That means not all Asians are geniuses, not all Indians like curry, not all Americans have guns, not all Australians have boomerangs, not all Koreans like k-pop, and we are all different. Once we recognise this and show respect to other people, this world will be a much safer, better place.

Social media, new trends, unachievable perfection and other things in the modern century have shaped us into a world where respect is rarely shown. People have lost respect for their friends and don't mind stabbing them in the back (metaphorically), lost respect for their teachers, their parents, their loved ones and everyone around them. Respect in this day and age is hard to come by, as most people these days are concerned about themselves. The troublemaker in class has become who they are claimed to be (a troublemaker) because of poor decisions and therefore, poor habits. When people get into a bad cycle, everything usually goes downhill with them. The older they get and the more disrespect they show, the more they feel the need to act out. These days, people have very little respect for others. People lack respect and decency for even the simplest of boundaries.

Karma can be seen as a superstition. But in reality, it's very real. We are treated the way we treat other people, and the consequences of our disrespect come back to bite us where it hurts the most. It's like Isaac Newton's third law of motion, where every action has a reaction that is equal in magnitude but opposite in direction. Like a mirror, the world reflects what you do back at you. When we are negative and do bad things to other people, negative things will eventually catch up with us. When we show disrespect to other people, whether it's not paying attention to a friend, doing something behind a family members' back, or otherwise show disrespect in any way, it will eventually find its way back to us. For instance, if you go up to someone and punch them in the arm, they may very well knock you unconscious if they're in a bad mood for the day. Saying something terrible to someone in the past can come back and haunt you in future. Telling someone that they are a failure may push them to be a better person. Next thing you know, you are applying for a job only to find out that they are the CEO. And well, I don't really need to explain if you're going to get the job or not.

Communicating in the right way is a great way to show respect to other people. A simple thanks, or a polite gesture can show respect to another person in a big way. Even just bringing them coffee can make a pretty big difference. But showing respect is a lot more than the odd coffee and talk in the kitchen at lunch. Showing respect to other people can be seen as an art, but it should come naturally to you now that you have come this far. A great way to show respect to someone is by first being optimistic. Seeing the negative in every situation reflects a poor self-image. Be bold and optimistic, seeing possibilities and being imaginative. If you're not the best at being imaginative, then be humorous. If you're not the best at being funny, then just be yourself, be who you truly are. Another thing about showing respect is that it's best shown with enthusiasm. If you are being handed a medal by someone who is completely bored out of their mind to an audience who is just about to fall asleep, you won't feel very respected, will you? If you want to show high-quality respect, be enthusiastic about it. But at the same time, don't be over-enthusiastic because that can easily get annoying. Nevertheless, always show respect as best you can.

Having a respectful mindset is all about positivity. Having a mindset that says "I will respect others because it's not only the right thing to do, but they deserve it" is an excellent sort of mentality to have. Maintaining this kind of thought process is the hard part. Some situations will throw a spanner in the mix of things. It may pour with rain just as you leave the tailor with your new suit on your way to your wedding. At this point, positivity is chucked right out the window and with good reason. But keeping a positive, respectful mindset at these times is where it's most important. This doesn't mean you aren't allowed to get upset or annoyed about something, it means making sure you don't stay upset or annoyed. Moments when we are angry and irritated help us appreciate the good times in life. Maintaining a consistent mood is difficult. Having a consistently positive, optimistic, sunshine rainbow sort of mood is close to impossible. We all have those days. And I don't need to explain what "those days" are because you could even be having one right now. Knowing that everything will work out in the end, and whatever needs to be will be, can help us maintain a respectful mind set on one of "those days".

Now my mind has drawn a blank suddenly, how do you spell respect?

CHAPTER 14: ADVENTURES OF THE TIME TRAVELLING BRAIN

Past.

Present.

Future.

Think of your past. Have you regretted not doing something or wished you could take back something you said? Ever feel like things would be different if you changed how you reacted?

I want you to think of right now, in the present. How are you feeling? What are you thinking about? Where are you? Who are you with? Take in all of your surroundings for a moment.

Think about your future. What goals do you have? How are you going to achieve them? Who do you see yourself with?

Just then, you took a look into your past, observed your present and visualised what you want in your future. People often discuss how to think and what to think about. But when do you think? Yes, that's right, it's not a misprint. When do you need to think? Do you always stay mindful of the past? Learning from what has or hasn't worked before? Or are you thinking about now? How you feel and what's happening right at this very moment around you? If not, then you might be thinking of the future. What do you need to do tomorrow? Who are you going to see tomorrow? Where are you having dinner next Tuesday? Now that I've finished bombarding you with all these questions, let's get into perspective. Typically, we think about where we have been, where we are, or where we will go. But when is the right time to think?

Memories are moments in time that stick with you as long as you can remember them. You might cherish memories of your youth: playing video games, going shopping, going through school, and worst of all, puberty. When we get caught up in the past, we can become stuck in that time frame, reminiscing the fond times we had out by the lake or at the shop corner. When we think of the past, there are also times that we would very much rather forget. A time where a best friend turned into a worst enemy. A time where we have been hurt by a dissolved relationship. Perhaps a time where we have been impacted negatively in some way. If we dwell on these sorts of memories in the past, often we can resurface or develop unhealthy grudges. We can begin to feel resentment, not only for other people but even ourselves. It can be both a blessing and a burden forgetting things. When we recall the past, we usually miss a few details here or there, or remember it differently to what actually happened. This is often a result of our differing perspectives and how they change after the fact.

Being stuck in the past means that you relive the same memory again and again, often over-analysing it in the hope of a better outcome. When people get stuck in the past, they can begin to neglect the present and ultimately the future. If they don't fire up the DeLorean time machine and get back to their time period, they can wreak havoc in the real world and change history as we know it! Now that is entirely from a fictional point of view. In real life, when we think of the past, we usually remember either the best parts or the worst parts of our lives. As soon as we begin to think of the bad times, we can suddenly feel regret or anger for not doing or doing something. Even though we live in the present, dwelling on the past can directly impact our lives now. For instance, you might remember what someone did that made you upset. Even though it was way back then, you could begin to have a negative outlook on the person now. Holding on to our past with a grudge can eventually consume us and hold us back in fulfilling our God given destiny.

Remembering the good times in the past can have a completely opposite impact on your life. Many people experience a midlife crisis at some point in their lives and express a great desire to feel young again. Some may call it travelling back to your better years, typically being years between late teen and mid-twenties. People may be slightly more nostalgic about their memories, reminiscing about their old hobbies and interests. This could then escalate to dressing differently or taking up a fallen hobby. Next thing you know, they seem like a completely different person;

acting, talking and dressing differently than they usually would. Don't get me wrong, there is no harm in wanting to feel young again. But:

"Today is the oldest you've ever been, and the youngest you'll ever be again." – Eleanor Roosevelt

Sometimes the most powerful moments in life are only meant to be experienced once. People have midlife crises to feel young again, feeling old on the outside but being young at heart.

Past living is healthy on some occasions because remembering memories helps us in the present. We have faster and more efficient technology, connecting the globe of very social beings. How do people live in the present, in the now? People begin to pay less attention to where they have been and what they have been through, ignoring lessons, hiding memories, and ultimately neglecting their entire past. When people only live in the present, they can experience some uninteresting results. They may adopt a distorted attitude, believing that today will be their last, so they had better get the most out of it. And one day this will be true. We need to take hold of every opportunity that comes our way, and not put it off. However, people then start to neglect their future, not acknowledging the impact their actions today have on their tomorrow, and the next day, and so on. This can become very dangerous, especially when people begin to put themselves in daredevil situations like their tomorrow doesn't exist.

Failing to acknowledge the past and neglecting the future can have dire consequences at the end of the day. Eventually, people who live in the now hit bedrock, the money runs out, no-one is willing to stand by them, and they wake up realising that there is still another day to live. At this point, only two options remain. They need to either change their thinking and turn their lives around or stay stuck in a rut and be miserable. When people hit rock bottom after living in the present for so long, they find a large amount of regret. It seems ironic that wanting to live without regrets generates different regrets not thought of previously. Regret for not planning for the future, for the relationships they have lost, the people they have hurt and the things they have done. Living in the now puts the past and the future under real threat. Hitting a point where there are no more parties to be had, no more money to spend, no more people to romance and no more things to do can be very destructive.

Getting caught up in the future can be just as bad as the present or the past. When we only think of our future, we tend to procrastinate and put things off. We usually use phrases like "I'll do it later" or "I'll start tomorrow". If you have a permanent sign that says free chocolate cake tomorrow, there will never be any free chocolate cake. If we are always putting things off, leaving things till later, and acting as if we have all the time in the world, time is going to catch up to us faster than we know it. When we get excited about the things we are going to do, the places we will go, the people we will see, and the smells and tastes we will experience, we can begin to neglect the present and the past altogether, being in a trance of what could be and what might be, but what isn't at this point in time. If you wanted to build a treehouse, you can't just think about the finished product and wait for it to be completed. When everyone waits, nothing gets done. Dr Seuss' 1990 children's book *Oh, The Places You'll Go* details what the waiting place is; specifically that people get very confused and start to travel to a useless place. If you're stuck in the future, you're only waiting for things to happen and not actually making them happen for yourself. You can't eat your cake without first baking it, because eating butter, eggs, flour, sugar and frosting separately would be disgusting.

Neglecting the past and the present can lead to some severe consequences. When we are stuck in the future, we often procrastinate. We say that we will do this later, or perhaps not say anything at all and just put it off for "another 15 minutes". This turns your 10am house cleaning into a 10 pm go to sleep and do it tomorrow. Delaying and putting things off takes you away from having more time to do the things you really want to do. Typically, we put off and procrastinate chores, housework, work-work, and things that we don't particularly like or enjoy. Finding silver linings in work can help you reduce procrastination. It may mean looking at the end product and working toward it as soon as possible or rewarding yourself after smaller milestones to get the big reward at the end of your journey. Living in the future will be very different compared to how we live now. We could have holographic televisions, robot butlers, floating cars, interplanetary travel, and everything else brought to you by the movie or gaming industry. But if your mind is stuck in the future, your life will come to a halt. If you continuously think about the end product and don't do any work, how can you expect to get where you want to be?

Remember what you have just been through in the chapter so far. Now you may be wondering, what do midlife crises and *Back to the Future* have to do with thinking? What is a time-traveling brain? When I talk about these things, I'm referring to the way that you think and the "tense" that you think in. We need to have the right thought processes regarding tenses and **when** to think. Do we think in the past, the present or the future?

When do you think? This is completely up to you. You can think in the past and relive memories, or you can think of the now and live for this moment, or you could think of your future and dream bigger dreams. But we can't let ourselves stay stuck in a single time to think. There is a general process of how we think.

> We need first to understand our current circumstances (this is the now side of thinking). What is your current financial situation? How is your love life going? Are you fit and healthy, or do you want to be better?

> The next step is remembering where you have been. What have you been through? Who have you met? How did you previously feel? Why did you make a specific decision or not?

> And finally, give some thought to where you want to go. Who do you want to be with? What do you want to be doing? Be specific about this part.

The rest is up to you. It may help you to write this down so you can weigh up the strengths and weakness based on your own circumstances.

Caught in a time where you don't belong can be very difficult. When we fall into the habit of daydreaming and thinking about the future or acting out as a daredevil and thinking of only the present or having a midlife crisis and thinking about the past, we not only impact our own lives but the people around us as well. Knowing when to think can be very confusing. You may have only realised recently that you suffer from past thinking, present thinking or future thinking. If you aren't careful, you might get caught up in a specific time period. Going to extremes within each instance can be very dangerous as each time threatens your life entirely. It could mean that you are so reckless and thinking about the present that you lose a possible relationship with a friend. It could mean that you disconnect from your family within your midlife crisis. Or it could mean that you neglect your work and only think about the results, not actually completing anything. Each time stream has its own dangers.

Future thinkers, present thinkers and past thinkers all have their dangers and demons to face, as it is with all people in life. However, there is a way of breaking free of time-centred thinking without completely rupturing the time-space continuum and bringing about the collapse of the universe. There is a way that we can think in all tenses. We can think in the past, the present and the future. Using all of our tenses can help us make the best of our lives. Let me break it down for you. We must:

-   Learn from our past and understand it without being caught in our memories for too long.

-   Acknowledge where we are, how we feel, and what our current circumstance is without being stuck in the now.

-   Think of our future and where we will go but not be caught in the habit of procrastination.

Utilising all three of these aspects of thinking can help us make the most out of every decision. When we learn from our mistakes in the past, see what is happening around us and have a clear vision of where we want to go, the only way is up.

Correcting our mindset and thought processes isn't as simple as flicking a switch. It is said that it takes you three times as long to relearn a skill that was initially learnt wrong. So, don't be too panicked if you don't get it the first time. Rome wasn't built in a day, and neither was the earth for that matter. It was actually created in 6. Getting back to the point, let's see an instance where this can be applied. Take eating, for example. Now it might be that I'm just hungry right now, but I'll use a food metaphor. If I prepare some hot soup to save me making it later, I am thinking about the future. When I see that it's too hot and it could very well melt my face off, I am thinking of the past by remembering a few burnt tastebuds from the last soup incident. Then I think of the now and cool it down slightly by adding cool water or waiting. Although this is a very simple example, it still retains its value.

This line of thinking can be vital for goal setting. For a brief moment, focus on your current goals and how you set them.

The first step in effective goal setting is being completely clear and specific with what you are aiming for. If you simply say, "I want to get a good car", that's simply not good enough. You need to be more specific. Do you want a sporty car or a family car? Do you want a two-seater, a five-seater or more? Whatever it may be, make sure you are completely specific with your goal. Write it down in detail.

Next, plan how you will achieve your goal. It may be achieving smaller goals along the way that help you get to the overall achievement. When you have done this, and have written it down, put it in a place where you see it every single day. It may be above your bed, on the bathroom mirror, on the fridge, or even as your lock-screen on your phone.

Finally, the best way to get yourself there is by being consistent. Make a habit of saying your goal every morning when you get up and every night before you go to bed. This way, you aren't falling into the trap of procrastination, but still not being stuck in the present.

Procrastinating and putting off your goal will not get you any closer to where you really want to be in life. However, keep in mind that your goals will change over time. You may aim higher and want to achieve more or even change your aim completely. Monitoring how your goal will benefit you is very important, however:

"A goal is not always meant to be reached. It often serves simply as something to aim at." – Bruce Lee

In saying this, we always need to have goals in our lives. Whether it's a long-term or a short-term goal, having something to aim at is very important. And sometimes you will fall short. Sometimes you won't reach your goals, and you won't make the cut. Just remember that even if you aim at the moon and miss, you will land amongst the stars. That's not to say that you'll be heading towards a ball of gas and fire if you fail to reach your goal, but you get the point I'm trying to make here. Reaching your goals will take time and hard work. But when you keep at it, be persistent and have a positive attitude, you will reach your goals.

Results are often more appreciated after hard work and a bit of blood, sweat and tears. Making sure you're reaching for the right goals is very important. When deciding which goal you're aiming for, you need to think of a few factors. How will this goal benefit you, both long term and short term? How important is this goal to you? Will my tense thinking be impacted in any way or used in achieving this goal? Time-based thinking is used in just about all cases where decisions need to be made, and the link between the way we think and the goals we have is crucial. The wrong thinking paired with the right goal can lead to failure, just as the right thinking with the wrong goal can lead to demise. You need to trust in your instincts, how you feel, what you think, and be prepared for all sorts of dangers and challenges. But you won't be alone along the way. I mean, having a time-traveling brain with you is pretty cool, right?

CHAPTER 15: HANDS BOUND

Tick. Tick. Tick. That's the sound of life ticking away. As you create both happy and sad memories, experience moments of anger and joy, feel love and pain, time is continuously escaping you. It does seem rather grim and extreme, but we are losing time. Especially when we waste time on useless things. On arguing over something so small and insignificant, getting upset on our daily commute to work, or complaining about not having enough. Time escapes us when we don't enjoy the moment. When we waste time on the small things or procrastinate and put off the big things in life, we are sacrificing the most precious commodity to ever exist on earth. When many people come to the end of their lives, they wish they had more time to do or say more. We need to value and cherish our time on earth while we still have it, using every opportunity we can to make the most of our lives. We can't get a refund on the time we have spent. For some people, this could mean the difference between life and death.

Insufficient time management is a very dangerous habit. When we don't manage our time well, we begin to build up a "later list", made up of things we put off until we have the time. Over our lives, we can become a slave to time, doing only what it says, when it says to do it. Most teenager's days begin with school at 9 am in the morning, finishing at 3:30pm, taking the bus home, doing homework (or not), having dinner, more homework (or not) and going to sleep. Then we wake up the next day and do it all over again, trapped in a constant cycle of time where the clock rules all. And it's not too different for adults. They wake up, go to work, come home and sleep, only to repeat this process over and over again, years on end in some cases. As time is the most valuable commodity, we have become slaves to it. We work our lives around time, and nearly everything has a set amount. When do you wake up in the morning? When do you get to work or school? When do you finish? When do you go to sleep normally? You see, our schedule is typically the same day in and day out because of our limited amount of time to do anything outside our usual rituals and routines.

Organising your life around set times is still important because it generates consistency and patterns within one's daily life. But how can we work with time instead of against it? You need to take hold of everything you do in your usual daily routine. At first, you may feel as though you are still being held hostage by the hands on your clock, but by changing your perception and reorganising your life, everything can be different. By planning out something new and exciting to do every once in a while, we throw a spanner into the mix, making our lives that little bit more liveable. It could be watching a movie with friends, spending a night out in town, going hiking or canoeing or merely trying a new experience. But be aware of this amazing yet agonising tool called a deadline. How can deadlines help me when they are the one thing I fear I won't meet? Deadlines are one of the most beneficial things to have in your life if you want to get something done.

Productivity is significantly maximised when we are close to a deadline. If you really care about your work and there is a deadline you need to meet, being put under a high amount of pressure can help you complete it. It does sound downright bizarre, so let me explain. You might get all worked up when put under pressure. If you channel this energy into work instead of stress, you can use it as a constructive force rather than a destructive force. Don't let the pressure that other people put on you weigh you down and get you all sad and moody. Instead, use it to your advantage and show that you are stronger than what you and they think. But pay close attention to where you're directing this energy and in what way you are directing it. If you focus it on proving that you are better than someone else, you're not focusing it in the right direction. Instead, focus on your productivity; on the smaller steps to achieve the bigger goal. I encourage you to review how you perform under pressure. This doesn't give you permission to leave your exam revision to the night before or the morning of the exam, nor does it let you leave your work till the very last minute. Too much pressure causes an explosive reaction. By planning out how you're going to meet your deadline, you can drastically increase your level of productivity.

Wasted time can never be taken back. We can't go up to God and say, "Hi, I'd like a refund of this day. I have my receipt. It was completely wasted on binge-watching TV and eating 13 packets of chips", because we aren't given a receipt. We can't be compensated for wasted time with a card that provides us with more. The doctor may say you have three months left to live, but you could get 15 years instead. The expiration date might say the 21st, but the milk really expired on the 19th. We don't know how much time we have left in our lives. That's why time is the most valuable resource man has ever known. It's more valuable than the most precious diamond or the largest amount of gold because you can't put a price on time.

Goals are often put aside and procrastinated about when we are stuck in a "now" mentality, only thinking about the present and neglecting the past and the future as we've discussed previously. When we procrastinate, we exercise poor time management habits, deliberately putting off important things so we have more free time now rather than later. When we put things off, we are only stealing time from ourselves. If we fall into the habit of procrastination, we may never reach our goals and aspirations. For instance, the person who emits all the symptoms of a cold or flu might put off seeing the doctor because they have work to do or a test to study for. At the end of the day, no test score or workload is more important than your health and wellbeing.

Motivating yourself is a hard thing to do. Some people don't have enough motivation to drive themselves. We need to snap out of it and get onto it right away. Stop wasting time, get off your butt and get going. Focusing on your goal can seem intimidating, but it's all a matter of perspective. Setting smaller achievable goals with specific time schedules and deadlines can make your life a whole lot easier. Consider it this way: the journey to your goal is like a wooden bridge. Every time you put it off, leave it for later or postpone it because you don't want to do it now, you are lighting the fire right behind you. Eventually, the bridge will burn up if you keep procrastinating and you will fall into the endless cycle of never being able to achieve your goal. We need to take hold of ourselves, break out and then stay out of the procrastination cycle. Don't hold yourself back from greatness, from success, from prosperity, from happiness and from whatever your heart may desire.

How do you maintain your focus? For starters, don't put things in your way to distract yourself. Stop completing side quests! Once you complete one, two more will pop up, then another four, then another three, and more and more until you completely forget about your main quest. Stop using things to distract yourself from your path to completing goals and fulfilling dreams. You need to concentrate on getting from where you are to where you want to be in the most efficient way possible. Without focus, how can you expect to get where your goal is? How can you expect to become fit and healthy when you distract yourself with cake and ice-cream? How can you expect to meet the love of your life if you never put yourself out there? How can you expect to pass the test if you don't know what the topic is? The journey will be tough. You are going to go through lots of hard times where you need a lot of hard work and persistence. Sometimes it's not the destination but the journey that makes it all worth it.

Journeys are full of ups and downs, highs and lows, mountains and valleys. You may get side-tracked, or be forced to take a detour, but that doesn't mean you stop going where you want to go. If you're going to achieve your goal, you first need to be organised. Being organised means you have a place for everything and everything in its place. Plan out your journey carefully and make sure you can visually see it. Productivity plays a big part in this. The higher your productivity, the easier the journey to your goal. Maximising your productivity can be quite challenging if you don't understand what's holding you back. You need to assess your situation from a completely non-bias point of view. You may want to ask someone close to you about their thoughts on achieving your goal or possibly how they would do it. This can give you another perspective on how your aim can be completed. Once you understand what's in your way, find strategies that help you deal with the hindrance or how to get rid of it. You may be trying to get some work done, but a new episode of your favourite TV show is just about to start, and the TV is just a chair turn away. You could simply shut the TV off and go in another room where there are less distractions. Or if you are tempted to go on social media or on your phone, leave it in another room while you work. Making these sorts of small changes can significantly impact your productivity.

Monitoring how you spend your time can be quite surprising to some people. What have you done today? How much time did you spend working? How much time have you devoted to social media? To the television? To your family and friends? Asking yourself these sorts of questions will help you see how much time you give to different tasks in your day. The best way to find out how you spend your time is by writing down everything you do in your day. It could go something along the lines of:

- Woke up at 6:30am. Went to work early for a staff meeting.

- Ate lunch at 12:30pm with Richard at the new burger place to try something new.

- Spent 45 minutes on the toilet playing Candy Crush.

Being brief but specific with your daily activity is essential. When you do note down what you do in your day, don't be afraid to be brutally honest with why you are doing it and how long you really spent on each task. The only person that should see this is you. Once you have enough data and have done this for a full week, reflect on the results. How do your weekends compare to your weekdays? Where are you spending the most time? Where should you be spending more time? Asking yourself questions similar to these can help you change your life and use time to your advantage.

Life is full of necessities and tasks with set amounts of time. We need to prioritise our days to make the most out of them. If you spend hours on social media but turn down dinner with the family, you aren't prioritising correctly. When we prioritise our tasks and things to do for the day, we might discover some free time here or there, or that there isn't enough time in the day to do everything. When you see some free time in your day, consider completing a task that needs to be done in the future. If you have tasks that you can't fit into your day or you don't get around to doing, write them down on a list. Throughout the next week, complete these tasks wherever you can. As you complete them, cross them off your list. If you come to the end of the week and you still haven't gotten around to some of these tasks, you have two options. The first option is to re-assess the importance of these tasks. If they have made their way to your "left-over list", then they shouldn't be at the top of your priorities. The second option is getting it done right now. Make this extra task your top priority, no matter what. This way you can eliminate it from your extras list and get it completely out of the way. Through this process, you can get the best results for managing your week.

One of the biggest time management mistakes is trying to fit in too many tasks into our day. Even though we may think up 20 different things to do, we may only get to 5 of them before midnight. If we cram too much into our day, we risk rushing what we've planned and missing out on some of the best moments in life. Then we come to the end of the day feeling disappointed that we didn't do everything that we'd hoped to do. Stop planning a million task for one day. Assuming we get a minimum of 8 hours sleep every night, we only have 16 hours in our day to eat, work and socialise. You may want to take a step back from all the rushing to plan out your time carefully. Never (and I repeat never) multitask two very important tasks. Although we think that it's okay to vacuum the house and call our sister in law at the same time, it's not okay. Even though we think that we can fold the washing, iron some shirts, wash the dishes and watch the latest episode of "Keeping Up with The Kardashians" at the same time, that isn't right. We need to take time to do set things in our day. If we try to do everything at once, eventually we'll explode. Don't waste time trying to do everything at once. Learn to prioritise, pace and manage your time.

Perfectionism is one of the biggest time killers and wasters in our lives. From personal experience, I know that perfectionism can waste an incredible amount of time. Even after spending hours upon hours trying to make something perfect, we often still aren't happy with it because everything can always be improved. Perfection can never be achieved in life. Instead of trying to make something perfect, we need to make it the best it can be, or at least the best we can make it.

Another major time waster is messages, calls and social media. These days, people are so caught up with the latest gossip about who's getting married, or who is having another baby, or if their friend got a new car. Realistically, you don't need to live your life on social media. You don't need to know what everyone is doing, every second of the day. Sometimes it's better to live in the moment. When you have "your face in your screen" as my parents say, you miss out on the beauty of the moment. You don't need to Instagram your lunch with #hungry or #cheesetoasty. Frankly, lots of people don't care about what you ate for lunch, and none of them can taste it with you. Now I'm not telling you to delete your social media accounts because they're pointless. I'm simply asking you to be more aware of where your time is spent, and how much time you spend on different aspects of life.

Scheduling time to complete tasks individually can help you avoid multitasking. But sometimes, we don't even know we're doing it. We see a message on our phone and feel that we are legally obligated to answer it instantly, while also watching the footy and cooking the barbeque for the family dinner or worse, while behind the wheel. Sometimes we instinctively answer our phone while trying to make lunch for the kids and clean the fridge. I'm not saying that doing two things at once is always super negative, but focusing on one task at a time never hurt anyone.

Why do we feel the need to multitask? When we do too many things at once, we risk the possibility to mess something up and not notice our mistake in the rush. Setting a goal to do one thing at a time and get it done the best way possible is one thing. Doing it is another. We can say we're going to become super fit and healthy. Then suddenly, we find ourselves returning to the same fast-food restaurant for the third time today and decide to start the diet tomorrow. Especially around November and December, people leave things for the new year saying, "oh I'll think more positively in the new year", or "I'll be healthier in the new year" or the mind-numbingly annoying "new year new me" sort of thing. Realistically, you don't have time to waste on waiting around for the new year. Get it done right now. Start today. Make the decision **right now** that you are going to eat healthier, you **will** build that treehouse, you **will** talk to your crush, whatever you may want to do, decide to do it today. Not tomorrow. Today!

Planning your day can be quite difficult if you don't know where to start. Begin by making a list of all the things that you need to do in your day. It could include having breakfast, work, getting the kids ready for school, whatever it may be. Now on a separate list, write down all the things that you may want to do, these could be grabbing lunch with a co-worker, or watching a movie with the family. Whatever your wants are, write them down. Next, you need to assign time to each of the tasks you need to do and prioritise them from most important to least important. I would advise allowing a few minutes in-between tasks as a bit of cushioning. Between meals and work, start at the top of your list and schedule in all the things you need to do. Once you've finished, you might see that there are a few things leftover that you just don't have any room for. If this happens, ask yourself if you are spending too much time on something and where you can cut back to fit more in your day. You may also have some free time left over. With this time, factor in the things you want to do in the appropriate time frames. This will ensure that your wants aren't getting in the way of your necessities. Once you complete this process for the rest of the week, you should have a full plan for the next 7 days. Alternatively, you may want to complete this process before you go to bed for the next day.

WARNING! Even though you may have a thoroughly

planned week ahead of you, full of meals, work, socialising and lazing around, don't get stressed if you don't follow each task to the minute. Take in your day as it comes. If you happen to finish something earlier or later, that's completely okay. I mean really, your hands aren't bound by time, are they?

CHAPTER 16: THE JURY VERDICT IS…

Judges are often portrayed to be large, brooding people with big wigs and a giant hammer, always grumpy and heavily biased. When people think of the word "judge", they immediately associate this with the image described. However, you don't need a wig and a hammer to be a judge. In fact, everyone is a judge because we all judge people. We judge them based on their looks, the way they act, what they wear, who they associate with, and every other aspect we see, as well as some we don't see.

Although we can have opinions about people, we shouldn't judge them. This means that you shouldn't criticise people based on their ethnicity, you shouldn't put them down because of what they have done, and you shouldn't go out of your way to be mean to them because of who you think they are. We aren't the judges in this world. Who are we to judge and critique other people? Are we the ones who decide everything in the world? What belongs and what doesn't? No. Does the world revolve around you? Certainly not. We need to break free from our negative, judgemental mindsets. At the end of the day, we are only in charge of what we do in life, and how we react to any situation.

Hurt. It's a touchy word that makes us remember a time where we have been hurt by someone or a group of people. When we judge others, we don't get to see the many repercussions after our words and actions. The old saying, "sticks and stones may break my bones, but words will never hurt me", is not true at all. When we say something hurtful to someone, it can have devastating impacts on them later on in life. Even if they choose not to listen, our words still impact them. Our judgement hurts us just as much as the people we judge. Over time, you can get into a negative habit of judging people and being mean, rude and insensitive. This can lead to the loss of many friendships and relationships based on your inability to stop judging people. Although thoughts and words cost nothing to say, they can be more valuable than many material goods in the world. When we judge others, we are not only dampening their life but making ours a lot less meaningful. The more you put other people down and say the wrong things intentionally to hurt them, the more likely you are to end up walking alone in life.

Blame is one of the main concepts associated with judgement. When arguing with others, we tend to twist and manipulate the facts to put the blame on the other person. We are more inclined to play the victim, thus putting them in the position of the villain. The role of the victim is simple.

- They are always innocent and couldn't hurt a fly.

- They know all the facts and everything they say is true.

- They have the right to blame anyone they want in any form they want to, be it on social media, in person, or otherwise.

You should never put yourself in the position of the victim. Even if it was their fault to begin with, you should never blame someone else. In many cases, the victim can be the one in the wrong, and because they've twisted the truth, they can manipulate people into believing their lies. Many people who play the role of the victim use various forms of manipulation to portray their innocence as well as the other person's guilt.

Hiding behind "they started it" is not only immature but very dumb. When we hear "I didn't do it", we can compare the person saying this to a child on the playground, telling the teacher what supposedly happened. The self-acclaimed victim places the blame on the other person, attempting to shift the focus from themselves to who they are accusing. When involved in an argument, we are more inclined to try and justify our own actions and put ourselves in the right. People may even go to extreme measures to ensure that they aren't blamed. Although you are taking yourself out of the firing line, being in the position of the victim is not a great place to be. In the end, doing the wrong thing will come back to bite you where it hurts. People who feel the need to blame others may do so because of their insecurity and inability to take ownership if they are in the wrong. We need to be aware of what role we are playing and whether it is right or wrong.

Perfection is the embodiment and unachievable image of social expectations. People find the need to say that others aren't perfect without looking in the mirror and questioning the things they do. No one is perfect, and no one will ever be.

Take a look at a story from the Bible. In John 8:1-11, a woman is taken in front of the crowd to be stoned to death for committing the act of adultery. The religious leaders said that the law of Moses condemns this woman to be stoned. When asked what He thought, Jesus picked up a stone and offered it to the crowd, saying that whoever is perfect should throw the first stone. Whoever has never sinned in his life and lead the "perfect" life deserves the honour for throwing the first stone at this woman. When considering their own sins, the crowd dispersed, and Jesus forgave the woman of her sins.

This story teaches us a very powerful lesson. We shouldn't judge people when we ourselves have flaws. We need to break free of the mentality that we are superior because everyone else is worse than us. We all have our demons, and unfortunately, some choose to let their demons consume them. The main point is that we shouldn't condemn others if we aren't willing to be condemned ourselves for all the wrong things we have done and will do in future.

If you pass by the supermarket, you might catch a glimpse of magazines with models who portray society's idea of physical perfection. Weighing the perfect weight, wearing the perfect clothes, eating the perfect diet and living the ideal life. We see people at the gym who can lift more than we can and think, "if only I could do that, I would be perfect". Unfortunately, this is wrong, because they are probably thinking the exact same thing about someone else, and so on and so forth. We all have somewhere to improve. There is always room to grow, if not in one area then another. There is no such thing as perfect. Once we all wake up and realise that everyone has their unique imperfections, the world will become a much less judgemental place. People wouldn't need to fear being criticised for what they wear, what they eat, who they associate with, or where they live. People who pursue an image of what they see as perfection are only striving to be someone else's imperfection. When we see ourselves, we usually only see the "bad". These are the parts where we can improve. You might have the perfect body but low self-esteem. You may have amazing public speaking skills but can't get close to anyone because you're afraid of getting hurt. Whatever your imperfection is, embrace it. This is what makes you unique and different.

Viewing the bigger picture can be hard to do when you're looking through a microscope, only seeing a small part of everything. Sometimes it's good to get into the details and discover everything about a small part of an issue. But it won't do you any good if you try to change a small part of the issue when you don't see the rest of it. Everyone's life is like a massive photo album, and every moment is a photo. If we only see one picture and not the whole album, we won't be able to respond positively. The repercussions of our response impact more than just a single person. What we do every day will impact how we live our tomorrow. The decisions we make today will change our frame of mind forever. Seeing the bigger picture isn't just about looking at the future, it's about looking at how far you have come with them and how much of your life they have been a part of. When arguments erupt between friends or spouses, it can often have drastic impacts on both of their lives whether they like it or not.

Egos only make arguments worse. When people bring their ego into an argument, it only increases what is lost on both sides after the dust has settled. Consider a time where you have brought your ego into an argument with someone. Did it end well for both of you, or did it fall apart after that? Although the results will be different in all cases, these testing moments in relationships can lead to a falling out. When we come to a tense time or feel uneasy when we are talking to someone, the last thing we need to do is bring in our ego. You can make sure that this doesn't happen by calming down completely. Take some deep breaths and assess the situation. You may even want to walk away from it and come back to it once you have taken the time to reassess the issue. When you do return to the argument, don't let yourself get all worked up and stressed. Stop blaming them and pointing out their faults. We all have some flaws that can't be fixed.

Negative and judgmental comments don't achieve anything at the end of the day. What did you get out of calling a person overweight while you were driving? How did you benefit from calling your co-worker stupid for a mistake they made? You might say it was just a joke and that you were just kidding around. The casual banter has its limits. Attacks about how a person looks, who they associate with, and what they do is completely wrong. We are all going through things in life and wish we were a little different. Other than a pointless ego boost, the only thing you get out of judging people is knowing that you hurt someone and that you're a terrible person. It's understandable if the rare insult slips out once in a blue moon because we can't keep a lid on our thoughts 24/7. But if you are continually splurging out "you're dumb", "you're annoying", "you're fat", "your hair is weird", "don't even get me started on you", then stop! Just stop! It's plain and simple. No three-step guide to stop being rude and inappropriate. There is no real need to judge people because it doesn't benefit you or them.

Judging people can turn into a very unhealthy habit. It can turn a happy-go-lucky person into a grumpy person. When we get into this habit, we don't even know we are judging people anymore. It becomes involuntary to put people down. So, how do you stop judging people? Other than just cutting it out and stop being rude, consider this if you're really struggling to be kind. Instead of insulting people, when you feel as though you're going to say something mean and hurtful, you can give them a compliment. Instead of saying "Hey you! Yes, you. You're a weirdo!", try saying something like, "Hey, just wanted to say, I like how different you are". And if you have trouble saying something nice to someone, don't say anything at all. Just keep it to yourself and don't let it out. Don't let your words bring the world down if that's all you have to say. Sometimes silence is more powerful than words. This doesn't mean that you give your partner the silent treatment. In any case, see a counsellor or a psychologist or something. When you feel as though you want to judge someone, exercise some self-control. Now, if you walk away from an argument and want to return to it without being judgemental, follow the simple J.U.D.G.E rule.

J: Justify the situation

Justifying the situation is the first step in not judging someone. Ironically, following the JUDGE method when you don't want to judge someone is the best thing you can do. You need to outline and understand the situation. What has happened and what are the real facts. Don't let your emotions cloud your thinking and bias your information. Being calm in your approach can help keep things cool. You need to do it with all honesty without trying to defend yourself. If you only try to explain yourself, you may as well let it get worse until it completely blows up, and both sides are left with casualties. Outline exactly what happened and why you believe it happened. But be careful! What you think happened isn't necessarily true. We all have different perspectives on a situation. It is also very common for people to exaggerate the facts and turn ten soldiers into 10,000.

U: Understand the other perspective and motive

Motives need to be understood if anything is going to happen by the end of this. You need to be able to understand the other sides perspective if you ever want to get anywhere. Our eyes are like a set of glasses. We see the world through a specific lens. If someone else gave you their glasses, you would see everything differently. If you see one side of it, you may say that the number is a 6. If you put on the other person's glasses, you might see a 9 instead. Regardless of whether it was meant to be a 6 or a 9, both perceptions interpret the information differently. Establish a base of what you know to be true, not what you think might be true. The true facts might surprise you. Understanding the other person's perspective will help you reach a conclusion and a solution that benefits both sides of the argument. When interpreting the other side, don't bring your own perspective and begin judging them on what they think the situation currently is. This is all done in a calm environment and mannerism, so that no fuses are ignited and things explode faster than you can say the word "guilty".

D: Don't assume anything

Assuming that you're still reading this and you're understanding the concepts, never ever assume anything when it comes to an argument. When you assume things, you create information which may be true or false. My parents always say, "don't assume anything, or you'll make an ass out of you and me".

If we assume the facts within a situation, we jeopardise a healthy outcome. When we assume things about people, we typically fill in missing information with facts that represent how we want to see them. For instance, if someone in your social group did something but you didn't know who, there would typically be one or two people you would go to blame first. In reality, it may very well be the person you least expect. When you try to control the outcome by assuming other people know information when they really don't, you can either underestimate or overestimate their capabilities. You may think that they can do something, only to find out that they fail miserably and blame you for it. The lesson is, never make any assumptions.

G: Get another opinion

Asking someone else for their opinion can go either of three ways. One way is that they agree with you and what you think about the situation. In most cases, this means that the person is someone close to you and will take your side regardless if you are right or wrong. Another outcome is that the person takes the opposite side. This may be a person that may not particularly like you or can get something out of it by siding with the other person. The third way involves reaching another alternative that appeases both sides. You need to be careful when you get an opinion from an external source. Remember that this is only an opinion, a biased perspective on the situation. If you begin to ask many people about what they think, you are only revealing how desperate you are to be right. Although you may ask for someone's opinion on the issue, you should never get a third party involved in the argument. If you are arguing with one person, it can be dangerous if you bring a third person into it. If you do ask for another perspective, be careful who you ask.

E: Express yourself

Expressing your personal opinion is the final step when you feel like judging someone in an argument. Remember to approach the situation in a calm and collected attitude. If you come back to them all guns blazing, you are no better than when you left. Keep your judgements to yourself, especially when you feel tempted to share it with a friend or family member. When you do share your judgements with people, you become a gossip, one of the worst kinds of people to be. Communicating constructive criticism is completely different from judging someone. Although the case, there is a ridiculously thin line between the two of them. Be careful that your constructive criticism doesn't come off as sarcastic and judgmental. Now after reading the evidence, evaluating all possible outcomes, the jury verdict is…

CHAPTER 17: DON'T BE A GREEDY MONKEY

Greed comes in many different forms. In most cases, majority of people's bad choices are often motivated by greed. It can be material greed, where you hoard and desire material items to fill a never-ending void. It could be mental greed, where you want to know everything about a situation when it's not necessary. It could also be social greed, where you must have all the attention because the world revolves around you. Being greedy can become intoxicating and take over a person's life. Once a person is infected with greed, they neglect the feelings of others so long as they benefit from their actions. Greedy people may appear generous, claim that they want enough to get by, or say that they don't want to be lonely and 'deserve' the attention. When greed seeps into a person's soul and takes over their actions and behaviour, their life takes a turn for the worse, generating a downward spiral in areas of financial, mental, physical and emotional stability.

Imagine you've just been kidnapped and taken to a remote location in the middle of nowhere. Your kidnappers are just about to put out a ransom for your life and ask you what price you want to put on your life You may say several hundred thousand or a few million dollars, or you could be unsure and still captivated by the panic of the predicament. Stepping back to reality, how can you put a price on your life? In many cases, we can't. We don't know what we will do in the future and what we will achieve. Therefore, we can't put an exact price on our own lives. Although the case, people find it easy to put a price on other people's lives, usually low prices but prices, nonetheless. When you choose to treat someone negatively and not give them the time of day, you show that you don't value or care about them. Every life is priceless, not worthless. We all have an incredible amount of potential for greatness. Despite having a rough plan of your years ahead, no one can ever exactly know what the future may hold.

Arms and legs are two of the most important parts of our bodies when it comes to general living. We use our legs to get from "A" to "B" in the best way possible, and we use our arms to pick things up, make things, play music, play sports and everything in between. The cost of a prosthetic arm ranges from $5,000 to $100,000 AUS, and a prosthetic leg can cost between 5,000 to 50,000 dollars based on the types of functions it can perform. Based on these statistics, how much are you worth? Are you worth a million dollars? Well, in actual fact no, you aren't worth $1,000,000 or even 2 million. You are worth far more than that. Your life is priceless. Determining your worth isn't as simple as calculating the amount you own.

What price do you put on your heart? How much is your happiness worth? Does your hate or love have a higher price? A heart transplant can cost up to 1.2 million dollars. Think about how much your brain costs. How much does your mental capacity cost? Your memories? Your habits? Your quirks? You can't put a price on someone's potential and therefore someone's life, without grossly undermining their worth.

Are you rich?

I'm not looking for any other conditions or additional information. A simple yes or no will suffice. Are you rich?

Now whether you have answered yes or no, I won't be able to tell. If you answered yes, then you are 100% correct if you refer to the correct type of rich. If you answered no, then you are (unfortunately) incorrect. The fact that you have read this far means that you have accumulated up to 16 full chapters of knowledge, not to mention the amount of personal growth you have experienced in your own life from before. If you said yes because you are rich in the money department, then that is not really what I am looking for in the question. The way people react to this question is usually yes or no based on their financial stability and current circumstances. But being rich is more than just having a comfortable amount of money in the bank. It means the amount of knowledge you have, how many memories you have and what they mean to you, the love that you have for your family and friends, and every part of your life that makes it worth living. Although there may be hard times in life, they help you appreciate the good times even more.

So, are you rich?

Efficiency and the ability to do something well is typically used to determine someone's worth in the workplace. If your worth is higher than someone else's, you hold more value in the company's eyes than the other person. But outside of work, what determines your worth? Is it the amount of money you have in the bank? No. Is it the number of friends you have? Definitely not. Is it the amount of knowledge you have? Yes! You just hit it right on the head. We need to focus on what we know and sometimes who we know. There is no use in having access to knowledge and not using it. When determining your worth, look at all you have been through, both the good times and the bad. Consider the significant defining moments in your life and how you responded to them. Your worth is one of the most important aspects of your life because it indicates the kind of life you have lived.

Positivity is one of the most valuable things you can have in your mindset because it's so difficult to maintain. Having a healthy, wealthy mentality may be the hardest type of mindset to uphold through the lows of life. You need to be able to stay motivated and be inspired to get back up and say, "hit me again". Life won't stop throwing things at you no matter how hard you try to stop it. This is why the strongest people in life are those who can cope with the pressure and deal with the hard times with the right mindset. Being rich in the mind is very different from being rich in the pocket. Some of the wealthiest people (materially wealthy people) began with nothing in their pockets but a mind full of wonder, imagination and ideas.

A great example is J. K. Rowling. In 2008, Rowling presented a speech at the Harvard Commencement. She stated that she was the biggest failure she had ever known, being the poorest standard of living without being homeless. In spite of all this, she had an idea. She had a magical world harbouring inside her mind. After she let it free in the world, she quickly rose to success. Despite having millions of dollars and being recognised worldwide for her iconic series *Harry Potter*, J. K. Rowling maintains a wealthy mindset which leads her to bigger opportunities to this day.

Detaching wealth from money and material possessions can be hard for some people to understand. We have become so used to knowing whether we are rich or not based on how much we have. People are truly rich because of what they know and who they know. People who create amazing memories with their loved ones, gain knowledge from reading and living life to its fullest potential are the wealthiest people in life.

What is the difference between knowledge and wisdom?

You might think that they're both the same thing. However, they are very much two different concepts. The ability to know something from reading the words on a page or observing it in action is what I consider to be knowledge. Wisdom, on the other hand, is the ability to apply this understanding on a practical basis in your own life. If you can talk the talk, you should be able to walk the walk. Sometimes we need to listen to our own advice instead of giving it to people who don't ask for it.

Types of Riches

Relationships are the first type of riches more valuable than money. But these aren't any old relationships. They're with the people that have come into our lives and changed it completely; the people that you have created amazing, funny, unique memories with. Those memories themselves are much more valuable than money. You can't pay a specific amount to feel happy or sad or thrilled. You can certainly buy yourself something or do something that would make you feel this way; however, the best moments in our lives are much more valuable than money.

Another type of riches more valuable than money is skills and talents. Each one of us has a special unique talent or knack for something. It could be singing or dancing, cooking or creating, swimming or soccer. Any sort of skill that sets us apart makes us rich because it makes us unique. The talents that we have should be embraced instead of shunned away. Some people choose to hide their talents or not embrace them because they don't want to feel different, and they "just want to fit in". That sort of mentality won't get you anywhere in life. You need to embrace your quirks, talents and skills no matter what they are. The fact that you can cook up a storm in the kitchen, or sing your heart out, or dance your problems away, or score the winning goal for your team, or write your imagination on paper, makes you different and rich beyond your wildest dreams.

Let me take you on a little adventure. In a faraway kingdom, a village was plagued by the excessive number of monkeys stealing their jewellery and food. The monkeys would come every night and raid all the local markets and houses for anything shiny they could find or anything they could eat. One day, a wandering stranger passed through this village. They begged him to help in any way he could. So, he decided to help the villagers by showing them how to catch these greedy monkeys. He tied a rope to a coconut that had a small hole in it. Then he placed a sparkly diamond inside the coconut, covered the rope and waited for his prey to spring the trap. A monkey soon came along and spotted the diamond in the coconut. It walked over to the coconut, reached its hand inside and held the diamond in its fist. But because it was holding the diamond, it couldn't escape. And because the monkey was so greedy, it was caught and shipped away to a land where there are no diamonds or jewellery of any kind. The village thanked the wondering stranger who continued on his travels. This story teaches us two main things. The first is how to catch a greedy monkey. But the second is not to be greedy monkeys ourselves. Sometimes we need to let go of the diamond to escape the trap.

Negative outcomes only follow a path to greed. Whenever we express an act of greed, we show how desperate we are to obtain something we may not deserve in the first place. The main form of greed is material. When we see a "massive" sale on something we want, we usually find every reason why we should get it immediately and overspend on something so pointless and materialistic. Then when we need money for the necessities of life like food, water, or electricity, we can't afford it because we just bought the new designer bag or the latest game. Next comes the stage where we begin to scrounge around for money because we "need" more. This is not to say that wanting something is wrong. It is to say that if we put something so meaningless in front of life's basic necessities or other people, we can find ourselves going down a very narrow rocky path. Many more menacing consequences come with greed, but hopefully, you will never have to encounter them.

We should never accept reasons or excuses for people to be greedy. You can't justify the risking of a person's life for a material good. There is no excuse for not caring about other people while you pleasure yourself with money, food, attention or any other negative habit people get into. Unfortunately, greedy people fail to realise that God provides for everyone when the moment is right. The bible says that God has our lives all planned out, knowing when we need something and why we need it. The trick is, God doesn't show us our life plan. He doesn't tell you you're going to miss your 2 o'clock meeting on Tuesday because you will be sick, but you will still be able to re-watch another Friends episode. When we fall into times of heartache and hit the lowest points in our life, God's divine plan will kick right in and bring you back to your feet so you can continue to walk through life with Him. However, He can only put His plan into action if we ask Him.

Monetary greed shows how much we value money over people in many cases. But why do we value money so much? Is it because it "makes the world go around"? Is it because we depend on it and fear losing it? In many cases, yes. People are scared of losing their money because if you don't have money, you can't provide for your family, your loved ones and yourself for that matter. People place such a high value on money that they treat $10 like $100. In some third-world countries, people get paid less than $1 an hour to do some of the hardest, most energy-consuming work. Many people exploit the desperation of the less fortunate for personal gain. These sorts of people know how to hustle their victims and leave them wondering where it all went wrong, being greedy people themselves. Sometimes it's not even other people. We can even trick ourselves into wasting our money away and later regretting it.

Survival of the fittest in modern society might not be easily identified. This is why it's important to have a rich mindset instead of a greedy one. We can employ a rich mindset by comparing our needs to our wants. Create two lists, one with all the things you need and the other with all the things that you want. Don't be afraid to be brutally honest with yourself when writing this list because only you should have access to it. This means that putting down "a new dress for the weekend wedding, so you can look better than everyone else" in the need column is not right. That is more of a want "to go and look better than everyone" (even the bride herself). Things that you need to survive and that are essential to daily life are put in the "needs" column. Once you know your needs for everyday life and your wants or the luxuries you would like to have, make a weekly budget based on how much you earn and your lists. After you understand your limitations, you need to make the decision not to give in to greed. Say it five times out loud in private right now just to be sure.

A greedy person is usually selfish, willing to do whatever it takes to get what they crave. At first, you might see many benefits of having what you want right here, right now. This typically means that you use present thinking, neglecting the future and finding yourself in an endless cycle of debt. However, selflessness also has its own benefits. When we give back to others or help them; otherwise, we feel better about making a difference in someone else's life. We are constantly given opportunities and open doors. But throughout life, doors will slam right in our faces and opportunities will be taken away from us. As another door closes, another one opens. Recognising this can help you through times where the door closes on us. Not getting that promotion can lead to you changing your job and being even happier. Not being offered an extra slice of cake means you won't find it hard to run after the robber who stole your purse. Not continuing in a relationship means you have an opportunity to meet the right person instead of staying with the wrong person. These are all just stories of sometimes and maybes. They can only happen to you if you choose to see the opportunities in your "problems".

Somewhere in the world, large financial transactions are being made. As each second passes, people get more and more greedy. After saying all of this, don't misunderstand and accuse me of saying money is evil. It's the intention behind the money that can make it evil. However, it can be used to do a lot of good in the world. Look at all the communities throughout Asia, the Middle East, America, Africa, Australia and all over the world that have benefitted from donations or people volunteering their time and efforts. If used in the right ways, money isn't evil, and it's not toxic to the soul. Money only becomes this way when we choose to do the wrong things with it and hoard it away from the world. This also doesn't mean that saving money is bad and having financial security is wrong. We all need to find that thin line between greed and financial instability where we can still do good for others but can survive ourselves. Once we understand where the middle ground is, we can help people realise that greed doesn't get you anywhere, and money isn't evil at all.

After reading this chapter and finding out about how greed can ruin your life, are you still going to be a greedy monkey?

CHAPTER 18: HOLY BOOK VS SOCIAL LOOK

Faith is being taken over by the media. But what is faith? Is it having hope in someone because they're your friend and you want the best for them? Is it understanding the bible and knowing all the psalms? The word itself means different things for different people. For some, faith is a way of life, but for others, it doesn't mean anything. In a practical sense, faith is defined as a sense of belief that is not based on any kind of proof, having confidence or trust in someone or something. Expressing faith in the modern-day and age we live in takes a considerable amount of guts and courage. Too often are people judged for being a Christian, or a Jew, or a Buddhist, or any other religion. When people share their faith, they are typically met with questions asking what the point of being religious is. What does Christianity have to offer? Being a Christian offers more than anyone can perceive or even imagine. Now I'm not telling you to convert or suffer the fire and brimstone. Everyone is free to believe in whatever they want to believe. But if you do feel as though Christianity is the religion for you, or even if you want to find out more, visit your local church and get in touch with Jesus.

Believing in something isn't always for everyone. Some people are atheists and choose not to believe in a religion. Some people are agnostics, choosing to neither believe nor disbelieve in any religion. There are also people who consider themselves as omnists, respecting and recognising all faiths.

What is your faith?

Are you Christian, Muslim, Buddhist, Jewish or something else? You may not even have a faith or religious doctrine. Regardless of your answer, a better question may be: where do you put your faith? And do people have faith in you?

You might have your faith in your family or your friends, your pets or your co-workers. However, it doesn't need to be in a living being. It could be in your car to keep running, your job to help you survive, your food to nourish you, your phone to help you communicate. Having faith in yourself is the most important place to have faith. When we don't have faith in ourselves, we can find that our biggest enemy is ourselves. It becomes easier for us to neglect the necessities in our lives, then slowly crumble and blow away in the wind. We need to have faith in ourselves.

Along with personality and circumstance, perspectives usually involve a fair bit of faith. Although it's important to have faith in the first place, we need to be careful where we place our faith. Having faith in the wrong place can mean the difference between good and evil. Faith matters! But not many people recognise it these days. People neglect their faith because of school, work, family, responsibilities or any other reason. Faith helps us make moral decisions. It may be what to eat based on our religion, it could be cheering on a friend even though they're in last place, it could be what to do based on what we believe. Everywhere in life, faith can be recognised and used to improve on life as we know it. Often in today's society, people are so caught up in Instagram-ing their lunch, keeping up their snapchat streaks or ranting on Facebook about how they feel about relationships even though they've been in way too many themselves. People have begun to neglect their faith, not seeing any benefit behind it. They don't see how it helps them if only they put in the effort.

Circumstances change many times in our lives, testing and challenging where we put our faith. The key is recognising where you can have faith and the different types. There are typically several forms of faith.

The first is religious. This is the usual faith most people think of when they hear the word. But as you may find out, there is much more than just religion behind faith.

Another form of faith is people faith. When people have faith in others, it is what I like to call people-faith which is (put simply) having faith in people. This form of faith is all around us, whether we like it or not. It is seen when a dancer has faith that their partner will catch them, when a sick person has faith that the doctor can help them, when we drive and have faith that people will do the right thing on the road (but we all know that doesn't happen). If you look close enough, where you have people-faith might just surprise you.

Circumstance based faith (as the name kindly suggests) is faith based on our circumstances. Most of the time, this form of faith will change based on how our circumstances develop. For instance, you may have faith that your friend will win a race, only to think twice once you see their competition. We need to learn to get rid of our circumstance-based faith and start embracing a people faith that is unconditional.

Every day, we are pressured to make decisions between what will benefit us temporarily and what will honour our morals and religious beliefs. People are constantly given a choice to please the social trend or please God, and unfortunately, the social trend is embraced more often. This is becoming more prevalent as people fall victim to the temptation to fit in with society. They want to look like everyone else, do what everyone else does, have the same things and go to the same places. Modern society has evolved to a point where religion is neglected, and faith is thrown right out the window. The constant battle between God and social trends resolves to a decision society would dictate. Even when we know that something is wrong, we still choose to follow social trends, inevitably leading us down dangerously unhealthy paths in life. It may not be the most apparent war being fought when compared to the recent struggles with terrorist communities and extremists, but the internal battles we fight are some of the most important in life as challenging as it is. Although at times it may not seem important, the results have substantial impacts on our way of life.

Decisions made throughout our lives are governed by our morals and what we believe in. However, these morals may not be what we were raised with. Over our lives, we make choices for ourselves about what we believe in and where we put our faith. But why are morals important? Think about your own morals and where you got them from. You might say you got them from your parents and being raised in a specific sort of environment. Others may say they chose their own morals based on their experiences or who they associate with. And still, others might say that they don't know. For those of you who don't know about your own morals, that's completely fine. Life is continually changing, making us develop new morals and drop old ones. Finding a set of morals is very important because it helps with consistent decision making. I don't mean what you're having for lunch or what you're buying at the store, I mean life-changing decisions like moving houses, changing countries, getting into serious relationships and mending broken friendships. If your morals are all over the place, you're more likely to make the same mistakes or further wrong choices because you see something you desire, not the details that stop you from getting there.

Society has evolved to a point where faith is being swept under the rug. People constantly hide their faith when things get tense about religion. They shun away from their morals and faith just to seem "cool" to other people, or to impress people who don't really care in the first place. The more you reject your faith, the easier it becomes. People get rid of their faith for their own reasons. They get all caught up and do something that they know is wrong because it benefits them or makes them appear as something they clearly aren't. Unfortunately, this is getting more and more common today. But alas, everyone has their limits. Some break under pressure and begin to persecute others based on their own mixed feelings on faith. We need to wake up to our own lives and see the importance of religion and faith. That doesn't mean you take a couple weeks off for a relaxing holiday to Hawaii for "meditation and inner peace". It's about evaluating where your faith is.

Socially, the classic stereotype of the current generation is not something to be overly proud of. Don't get me wrong, there are some young people in this generation that have achieved amazing things in their lives and have made great impacts in the world. But for the vast majority of my generation, there is a negative stigma against us. It's what I like to call the self-gen, which is short for the selfie-generation. People these days are so obsessed with their smartphones, along with being grossly addicted to social media. My generation typically has our heads in our screens, always online, never being social, not talking to people face to face, and living a completely virtual life, using hashtag after hashtag, wasting hours upon hours of our lives on the many forms of social media out there. While other generations may be busy working at their jobs and providing for their families, many in my generation are drinking, getting into drugs, illegal activities, wanting to be adults when they're only 13, wanting the most likes on their new profile pic and the list goes on and on. It will probably go on forever, depending on how extreme my generation really goes with their antics.

Uncommonly embraced in gen Z, religion is dissolving and dying out in the 21st century. Younger people are neglecting their religion and their faith. They do whatever they want, and at the end of the day, they don't care who judges them. After all, we are here for a good time not a long time, right? People don't realise how their actions today will impact their tomorrow. They spend their time on meaningless activities and getting into all sorts of trouble because as many would say, "why not". I think the better question is "why in the first place?". As each second ticks by, religions of all kinds are losing people to the harsh expectations of society. When I turn on the news, typically I will hear of a car crash, a home invasion, a crime, or some sort of big issue that involves adolescence or young adults. I'm not saying that we live a completely restrained life, not setting a foot out of line. We all deserve to live a little. At the same time, where are the limits? Where do you draw the line? Where are the points when it's gone too far? For many people, they don't know. Religion and faith can help us find these limits and turn our lives around.

Seeking faith or wanting to find your faith is a huge step in anyone's life. Having the initiative to say that you want to reconnect (or connect) with God is a major achievement. But how can you find your faith? First of all, you need to get a good understanding of what faith is all about. You can do this by reading the first part of this chapter. Great job! A+ for effort. Now comes the harder part (well, harder than reading words off a page). You need to go out and explore the different faiths in the world to find the right one for you. You might borrow a book on Hinduism, talk to someone about Christianity, look up a website about Taoism, there are hundreds of different religions out there. One of the easiest to find is Christianity. Now before we delve into Christianity, let me establish something. I believe that it doesn't matter if you are Catholic, Protestant, Methodist, Greek Orthodox, Anglican or any other denomination of Christianity. If you believe in God and Jesus Christ, and you want Him to be a part of your life, you are a Christian. The best thing you can do if you want to become a Christian is to go to your local church and talk to one of the pastors or priests about becoming a Christian. No one is turned away from Christianity, no matter how hard they try. Everyone will always be welcomed and accepted with open arms.

Separate from what I've said before, feel free to explore the other religions in the world. But for now, let's just focus on Christianity. In Christianity, God loves us no matter what. His love is everlasting and completely unconditional. You may be thinking, "how is this possible? How can someone love me even though I'm not perfect?". Well, that's the beauty of it. God loves you unconditionally because He knows that you're not perfect. He knows that you have your faults and imperfections. That's exactly what makes you human. That part of us that makes mistakes; that doesn't always do the right things; that does wrong things; is what makes us human. People might just say, "how can you believe in the unknown?" or "how can you believe in something if you can't see it?". That's what faith is all about. Believing and having faith in God even though you can't see Him is why Christians are so strong in their faith.

"If you go through life believing in God and He's not real, then you have nothing to lose because you have gone through life doing good. If you go through life believing in God and He is real, then you have everything to gain. But if you don't believe in God and He is real, then you have everything to lose." –
Blaise Pascal

At the end of the day, all we have is God.

Sometimes you won't know what to do once you've found your faith. Taking the first step in becoming a Christian could mean getting baptised, praying with someone close to you, or taking part in reconciliation. The church is the best place to do all this if you really want to make a full commitment to God. This doesn't mean you become a priest in your local parish and preach the gospel every Sunday. Maybe, but not necessarily. It means that you need to act upon your understanding of Christianity. You might need to change your life based on your new set of morals. But if you slip up and do something wrong, don't be afraid that God will smite you with a mighty lightning bolt (he likes to use floods and plagues instead). God is forgiving. He understands that you will make mistakes and that you aren't perfect. For that reason, He can forgive you of your sins instead of letting them drag behind you. But at the same time, that doesn't give you permission to be reckless and do all the wrong things on purpose. It means that when you do make a mistake and fall, Jesus will be right there by your side to pick you back up and walk with you all the way.

Understanding other people's faith can be difficult, especially when it clashes with your own. You might believe in one thing, but out of the 7 billion people in the world, there is probably someone who believes the exact opposite. When people get stressed, anxious and angry about a clash of beliefs, they get into more and more arguments with others about why their faith is better. More specifically, these arguments stand to justify why they are wrong, and you are right. These sorts of arguments are fuelled by a common inclination to be better than everyone else. You can't change a person's beliefs for them, say they are wrong and "prove" you are right all at the same time. In all honesty, it's not up to you to decide who believes in what. If we understood that everyone is entitled to choose to believe what they want to, we would live in a much more peaceful world. We need to learn how to understand other people's boundaries and other people's faith. Once we begin to discriminate others because of what they believe in, we only damage ourselves just as much as we are trying to damage them. We can't control what other people do and what other people choose to believe in because we live our own lives, not theirs.

Sharing your faith and expressing your spiritual feelings to the world can be quite daunting. Especially in a world where difference is shunned away, and anything that is out of the ordinary is rejected, you may feel scared to embrace your faith in your day to day life. What if someone sees me praying? Won't they think I'm weird? Why do I need to do it in public? My relationship with God is my own, not for the public to see, isn't it? If you are asking yourself these sorts of questions, banish them from your mind. You don't have the time to waste on useless thoughts. Not to be rude, but you shouldn't care what other people think of your religious beliefs. If you really are religious, truly religious, you will stick to and be proud of your beliefs no matter what.

Making an impact in the world becomes easier through faith. It may be through small actions like praying with a friend or saying grace before you eat your lunch in the office, or even praying for the paramedics in an ambulance and the people they are caring for. However, it could be as big as going on a pilgrimage and helping the less fortunate in the name of God, or even volunteering at your local charity. Whatever it may be, it is completely up to you and your religion. Sharing your faith with the world may be daunting at first, but that's why we have God to comfort us and be with us through thick and thin.

Faith is one of the best things in life that can drive you all the way to success. But success means a lot of different things to a lot of different people. It could mean achieving your dream job, or finding your soul mate, or going on a world trip, or finding inner peace. Faith can motivate us. Not necessarily religious faith (which still does the trick) or person faith (which also does the trick), but self-faith. Having faith that you can do anything will drive you to success. As soon as you begin to doubt yourself, you begin to hold yourself back from success. Along your journey, people will tell you that you can't make it, that it's impossible, or that you just aren't fit for the job. If you ever hear something like this, give some thought to these people:

> Michael Jordan was cut from his high school basketball team because he was deemed "not good enough".

> Walt Disney was fired from Kansas City Star because he "lacked imagination and had no good ideas".

> Henry Ford's first two companies failed, and he went bankrupt 5 times.

> Elvis was told that he was better off going to Memphis and driving trucks.

> Thomas Edison got fired from Western Union for spilling acid on the floor while conducting a secret experiment.

> Steve Jobs was fired from his own company.

> Bill Gates dropped out of Harvard University.

> Albert Einstein didn't speak until he was four years old and didn't read until he was seven.

All these people prove that having faith in yourself, trusting in your talents, being persistent, and having hope can drive you to success. So after all of this, who will win in your eyes? The holy book, or social look?

Take It From A Teenager

CHAPTER 19: LIVING LIKE THERE'S NO TOMORROW

Imagine you're in a grand church, with rows of people wearing black as sombre music plays in the background. You see people you know (co-workers, friends, family), all in despair as you walk up the middle aisle. A photo of you sits on a chair, surrounded by flowers. You go and sit in the front row. Right now, at this very moment, you are attending your own funeral. The priest invites your parents, then your spouse, then your best friend to say a few words about you. What are they saying?

In your mind, they may say all good things, or maybe all bad things (in which case it's rarely unlikely). They speak about how they have seen your life, how you've impacted them through your presence, and how they feel now that you are no longer with them. In this moment, you are visualising the impact you have made on the world. The eulogies you've just imagined represent how you see the changes you've made in other people's lives. This small exercise that you've just completed will help you understand how important your life really is and what you mean to yourself as well as the people around you. So, what do you want people to say at your funeral?

Regret is a heavy burden to bear at the end of one's life. A study was conducted in a hospital where 100 patients on their last breaths were asked what they felt when they looked back at their life. They said they felt regret. They didn't feel regret for the things they did in life, all the mistakes they made or all the things that they did wrong. They felt regret for the things they didn't get to do. They were held back by the fear of the unknown, fear of the next day, fear of how people will react, and fear of change. They regretted all the things they didn't say to someone they loved, the things they didn't do with people they hold close, not listening to those who really needed it, or not speaking up for those without a voice.

When you look back on your life right now, no matter how old you are, what do you see? You may only see the good times and the times where you felt like you were on top of the world. But look further than that. See all the bad things in life. The times you struggled, times you wanted to give up, times you did give up, times you regret doing something and wanting to take it back. When you look back on your life, focus on all the people that you have impacted. Look at everyone that has come into your life, whether they are there still or not. How have you impacted them? You may feel pretty bad about what you have done, or good, or perhaps disappointed that your life wasn't all you'd hoped it to be.

That is what this chapter is all about.

Every person has a beginning. We don't get to choose what it is, where it is, how it goes, and who is in it. All we can do is let the people around us help us in our own beginning. When we feel as though our life is nearly empty, we need to stop trying to find a way to change our beginning and start trying to make a better ending. Living a full life can mean a lot of different things to a lot of different people. The experiences we share, the things we do, the people we meet, the places we go, every part of our lives can be changed to fill us with the overwhelming glory of a full life. However, be warned: living a full life can take its toll. When people live their lives in a specific way, it can be devastating for them when they're brought back down to earth. Yes, living it up with a full cup is fantastic, but what happens when your cup is spilt by some bad news? It's very important when we go through life to live it up but still keep perspective on what's really important.

Wait! What about destiny? Where does that come into our lives and how does that apply? Well, I'm glad you asked. Finding your destiny can be quite difficult to do. Sometimes we don't even know what it is until we've already completed our journey. Some people never reach their destiny in life, being too preoccupied with minor things. That's not to say things like dental appointments, jobs, hobbies, etc aren't important. But when searching for our destiny, we need to stop looking for the right answers and start asking the right questions.

Finding your destiny will not be as simple as walking down the street and then POOF! "Oooo look, I found my destiny"! It's not going to be completely obvious and just spring up out of nowhere. Most of the time, it's a slow process, easing into your life gradually.

It could begin with a simple thought, then grow into a grand idea that could revolutionise the world as we know it. It could even be passed down to you by a family member or a friend. We all have something greater to achieve that fits into a universal plan.

Look at the word "universe". It's made up of two parts, the first being "uni", meaning one, and the second being "verse", meaning song. Each of our lives is like a single note in the grand song of the universe. In this way, all of our destinies are intertwined and connected to one another. We only get one note, and it's up to us to make sure we get it right, to fit into the full song so to speak.

Asking the right questions is far better than looking for the correct answer. Because when you look at both, it's clear which one is easier to work with. For instance, if the answer to my question is 3, what is the question? It could be anything really. It could be how many points on a triangle, or what is 1 + 2 equal to, or how many little pigs escaped the big bad wolf. Any of these questions have the one answer of 3. But once you have the right question, then you will know if the answer is right for you. If I ask you what's 1 + 1, you clearly know the answer is 2. It's not 11, it's not a window, and it's not 1. Asking the right questions in life are far more important than just looking for the right answers. Sometimes, you will find an answer, but it won't be for the right question.

Throughout your life journey, there will be major moments where you need to evaluate whether you are asking the right questions. These defining moments will be different for everyone. It could be marrying your spouse, having your first child, driving for the first time, or meeting your life-long best friend. Those sorts of moments are the times where people have come into your life, or you have made an important decision that has changed your life forever.

Where have you been in life? I don't mean Hawaii, New York, Tokyo, Shanghai or any other city out there. Nor do I mean if you've been to the mall, George's house, the bathroom, the kitchen or any of those places. When I ask you the question, "where have you been in life?", I mean "what have you left behind and what impact have you currently made on this world?". You may not think you've had a major impact at all. You might think that your life is pointless, and you are just here to live, grow old and die. If you are thinking that, SNAP OUT OF IT! Each person's life has a purpose in this world. We can find out what this purpose is by first understanding our past. All the memories you have of your childhood, of the people you have met, the places you have been, the things you have experienced, make up the answer to "where have I been?"

You may not fully understand where you've been and what you have achieved. That's completely fine. If so, you need to find out soon. If you don't understand what you have done and where you have been, how can you define where you want to go? Knowing that you can change yourself based on what you know is pretty awesome. Really think about it, where have you been in life?

Knowing where you are right now is the second step to discovering your purpose in life. If you don't know where you are now, then take in the current moment. Where are you (physically)? What is around you? Who do you see? What are you currently doing other than reading this book? Take in just this moment. Think about everything that you are today. It could be anything in your life that you feel is essential. It could be what your job is. It could be your family and friends. It could be what your typical daily routine is. Understanding all this is important in discovering your purpose in life. Your skills, relationships and perspective all play a significant part in the "now" section of your destiny.

What you know now is important because it will help you understand what you still need to learn. We all have something more to learn, regardless of how much we know already. We are continually learning as we go through each moment in our lives, meeting new people, doing new things and having brand spanking new experiences. Even by reading this book, you are learning something new every page of the way. Or should I say every word of the way? Answer me this, where are you now?

Understanding where you want to go is the final step to finding and defining your destiny and purpose in life. This can often be one of the more confusing steps out of the three, as many people don't really know what to do next. They get to a "now what?" point in their lives. Find another goal and dream! You need to get back out in the field and keep swinging. Don't get me wrong, we all take a swing and miss sometimes. But by the end of it, hopefully, we will look back at all the home runs we've hit and feel proud for even having a shot. We always need something to reach for and work towards. Otherwise, we won't get anywhere in life.

Take sharks, for instance. They have what is called a swim bladder. This means that they need to be continually moving to survive. Otherwise, they will sink to the bottom of the ocean. Like a shark, we need to be constantly moving, constantly getting closer to our goal. Once we achieve it, find another goal. It could be entirely out of reach, but you need to keep moving.

"You know what you got to do? Just keep swimming. Just keep swimming." – Dory

When looking at where you want to go in life, look at how that goal will change your life and impact the world for the greater good. If not the world as a whole, then how about your own world?

Discovering your passion and purpose in life will take you down some rocky paths. It's not going to be as easy as 1, then 2, and finally 3. You are going to need to go through some hard times, some challenges and some trials that will test you on how much you really want to achieve your goal. Being open to new experiences will make these times a lot easier. Many people are stuck in their own ways, only doing what is in their comfort zone and never taking a risk. When they do try something new, it may backfire, and they vow never to try that new food, or go down that road, or do this or that because of something negative they experienced. Sometimes it's the right thing to do if something bad happens. There is a chance that it will happen again. At the same time, things change.

"There is freedom waiting for you on the breezes of the sky, and you ask, "What if I fall?". Oh, but my darling, what if you fly?" — Erin Hanson

When you open yourself up to new experiences, there will be times where you won't like the outcome or the journey. That's exactly why you need to keep on keeping on. Each time you want to give up, give in or just stop in your tracks, push yourself to go beyond your limits. It will only make you stronger and get you closer to your goals. Think about your favourite food. You didn't always like that food, because there was once a time where you had never tried it before. But because you were open to a new experience, you tried something new, and now that meal has stuck with you all this time. Be open to new experiences and make the best of every opportunity that comes your way.

Pursuing your purpose in life is the most important thing in the world because you are very important. Whether you know it or not, what you do matters to many people. Most people think that they aren't important; that they haven't achieved anything; that they don't have any special talents or gifts. There is more to life than just being here to fill up space. We all have a purpose in life, which is to make a mark on the world. For the song of the universe to be complete, it needs your note in it. Making your mark is the most important thing you need to achieve in life. You may not know it yet, but you could have already made your mark. The people you have relationships with are greatly impacted by the things you do and how you live your life, one day at a time. Living like there's no tomorrow means that you take hold of every opportunity and get the most out of every challenge and obstacle you face in life. The mark that you make in the world will be what people reflect on at your funeral, what people will say about you and why they will say it. The world may be full of bad things, bad people, bad experiences, and sometimes bad decisions. But that doesn't mean we lose hope and give up on changing the world.

"If I can change, and you can change, everybody can change." – Rocky Balboa

Actions and the things we do often have much greater impacts on the world we know today. This happens through a ripple effect, where a single droplet can create multiple ripples in a large body of water if given a chance to do so. That's because every action generates a response from multiple audiences. It is said that a butterfly can flap its wings on one side of the world and cause a hurricane on the other.

The things you do have a greater impact than you may think. It could be a simple smile or a friendly hello that brightens up someone else's day, putting them in a good mood. Next thing you know, they are changing the world and making better decisions all because of one smile. It could be a small gift that you give to someone who means the world to you. Next thing you know, you are part of a happy family with three kids, two dogs and a parrot that won't stop screeching. You see, everything we do in this very moment has a much larger impact on the world we live in.

Caution! Living every day like there is no tomorrow has its limits. When I say that we need to live every day like it will be our last (because one day it will be), that doesn't mean we live wild, dangerous and irresponsible. Daredevils are fuelled by their hunger and thirst for adrenalin. These people will constantly put their lives at stake just to get a thrill. In reality, one wrong move could be the death of them. When we are living on the edge, sometimes a small action will push us over. It could be not properly preparing for something completely outlandish and crazy. Then suddenly, you jump out of a plane and pull the cord, only to release your lunch into the air instead of a parachute. We need to keep everything in perspective when we begin to push our limits and live close to the edge. That being said, it doesn't mean that you live in a bubble and don't do anything exciting. Having the drive to do something exhilarating isn't wrong either. However, we need to understand where our limits lie and when to get back to earth using the stairs, not jumping off the cliff.

Planning out all the days of your life is impossible because we don't know what trials and challenges will be in our way. When we get stuck in a rut and stop in our tracks, what do we do? Do we scream, yell and throw a tantrum? Do we crawl up into a small ball, hyperventilate and rock back and forth in the corner? Do we just give up on it all because there is a little bit of work to be done? No! We don't do any of that. We will be faced with a seemingly impossible challenge, eventually. We just need to have a little bit of faith and keep our cool. In the end, if it is truly your destiny and your purpose in life, God will provide, sometimes in the most unlikely of ways. God watches over us all and sees where we are going to struggle, where we are going to complain, and where we are going to want to give up.

When you get stuck in a place where you can't see any hope of it getting better, and you seem to have hit rock bottom, God will extend His hand to you. All you need to do is take it and let Him pick you back up. You might see it as divine intervention, finding hope where before, the only choice was giving up. Hope is what drives you to break through all the barriers to achieve your goal.

Work and the unnoticeable things we do every day can hold us back from our own lives. It sounds peculiar but devoting all your energy and hard work into your job can hold you back from your true purpose in life. However, you need to be careful about this. Sometimes, our calling is to work at our jobs. But for people who have goals and dreams to do more than just sit at an office desk all day, work can be holding them back. Now don't go ahead and quit your job first thing in the morning, move to an exotic location and "go find yourself". Definitely not. But when all you do is go to work, come home, and do nothing else, not having something to reach for and something to achieve, your job is holding you back from your true potential in life.

Sometimes we even hold ourselves back. You might think that "I'm risking too much", "never mind", or the classic "I'll do it later". You're only holding yourself back from your destiny. Be prepared to be bold and take risks. Don't be afraid of taking a few hits here and there. You need to be able to suffer through the pain to get where you really want to be.

Sometimes others will hold you back from your destiny. They might say, "you'll never do that, it's impossible", or "nah, it's okay, you don't need to do that", or even "it's alright, it just wasn't meant to be". First of all, that is their own opinion. Don't let anyone hold you back and tell you that your destiny is impossible. Achieving your dreams and getting in touch with life is never impossible.

Sometimes, opinions can be the one thing that we can't ignore, and they can really get under our skin. What would other people think of me if I did this? What would they say if I did that? To be honest, you are living your own life and not theirs. Not to be rude, but who cares what they think? Go out and make your mark on the world. Your friends might be concerned and try to put you down, and some people will try to pull you back to the standard, the mediocre, the normal, the satisfactory. But you are destined for more than just the norm. You are destined for greatness, for big things out there.

"You've gotta dance like there's nobody watching, love like you'll never be hurt, sing like there's nobody listening, and live like it's heaven on earth." –
William W. Purkey

That means you need to take hold of the day and make use of every single opportunity that comes your way. Make the most out of the moment and make your mark on the world, no matter how big or small. Change the fate of humanity forever! That seems somewhat deep and scary, but don't be afraid. Never fear the unknown or fear change. Change can bring about new things in your life, and the unknown can take you to amazing places. You need to go out today and live like there is no tomorrow.

CHAPTER 20: DESTINED FOR GLORY

Searching. At some point in our lives, we find ourselves searching for our passion, because we aren't born with all the answers. There's no manual for life, and it's never an easy 1, 2, 3. There will be moments where we stumble and fall, where we are down in the dumps and even times where we don't know what to do next. The answer to such a predicament comes from pursuing your passion.

We all have passions in our lives; the activities we love regularly doing. It could be singing or dancing, creating or drawing, stamp collecting or decorating, cooking or just looking, we all have some things in our lives that we are passionate about. But sometimes, we mistake hobbies for passions, not knowing what our true passions are.

What are your passions? It could be anything that you find comfort in or that you always come back to when everything has fallen apart in your life. If you don't know, then you have been blessed with the opportunity to find out. Once you do know what your passion is, never let anyone take that away from you. Hold on to it, because it's Gods greatest gift to you. When you begin to use your passion, you'll find that it can lead you to a very rewarding and successful life. After all, you are destined for glory and greatness.

Personal dreams and goals can keep us powering on through life. As you already know, at the end of the day, we all have our own destinies. We all have something that we need to achieve to make our mark on the world. You may have already made your mark on the world without even knowing it. It might seem quite daunting at first; knowing that any move we make and major decision we take can change the course of human history to come.

Sometimes we may get confused with our destiny and that of someone else's. It may not always be our goal or dream that we are reaching for. It may be someone else who uses our progress to fulfil their own destiny. If it does happen in your lifetime, we need to be humble and let them take hold of it. Every destiny is essential and vital for humanity. It will take some patience and persistence, but eventually, we will learn to understand what our true destiny is.

When searching for our true passion, Positivity is important to maintain. If we aren't positive, we risk letting the demon of doubt into our minds, infecting us with uncertainty and paralysing us with the fear of the unknown. Chances are, you won't recognise your passion instantly. Some people need time to see where their passion is, while others need help with their uncertainty. Don't get me wrong, it's great to have multiple passions in life and having several things to excel at. But be careful not to rush into a passion. For instance, before you think your passion is cooking, try to cook something first. You may, in fact, find that after attempting to create a gleaming 5-star 3-course meal, all you can really cook is eggs and toast and discover your passion for eating instead.

If you do find that you're unsure what your passion is, go out and try something new. You have nothing to lose and everything to gain in a new experience. If it's your passion, then pursue it. But if you find out it isn't, at least you aren't heading down the wrong path in life. Knowing your real passions is the first step in using them for your benefit.

Passion itself is defined as any powerful or compelling emotion or feeling, such as love or hate. In this instance, I refer to passion as something we love and are driven towards. But what happens if we don't have it? Do we just exist without meaning? Do we just sit here and do nothing for the rest of eternity? No! Definitely not! Passion is one of life's greatest gifts and sharing it with other people is even greater. Its absence is a burden in one's life because, without it, we don't have meaning. Without meaning, we have no direction. And when you have no direction, you will become lost in a sea of doubt, despair and the worst parts in life (also complete and utter boredom).

The word passion comes from the Latin word "passio" which implies suffering and the endurance of hardship. To be truly passionate about something means to fully commit to it no matter what is thrown at you, despite all the pain and loss you may encounter. Without suffering, how can we ever expect to grow? Without hard times, how will we understand what good times really are? And without passion, how can we truly live our lives to their fullest potential? Passion is vital to our existence.

Closing yourself off from your passion not only means that you are disconnecting from life, but you are also disconnecting from God. We have all been blessed with our passions by the Lord our God. If we choose to reject this gift, how can we expect to please Him? By embracing and holding on to it, we can soar to new heights and become closer to God. They help us fulfil our purpose. We need to find them, understand them, and use them to fulfil our destiny.

Passions may be neglected, left as unknown because people don't pursue them, or they begin to follow negative habits. The true potential we hold is only known by God, despite what others may say or think. We can't afford to let it go unnoticed because they are our ticket to success, our means of getting to the top and looking out beyond the horizon.

Jobs aren't usually seen as the most fun things to do during the week. Many people wake up at 7 in the morning, take the bus or drive to work and sit at an office all day until 5pm. They then get stuck in traffic for an hour, only to come home, eat and go back to sleep. This is a constant loop for some people, which can get very dull, very fast. People with a bored mentality, only working to pay the bills, often live bored, tired lives that don't have much joy or happiness. But when people find passion in their work, or they find a place where they can use it in their jobs, it no longer becomes work.

These people experience a feeling of achievement, knowing

that what they do is worthwhile. They know that their job is benefitting them more than they know because they are getting paid to do something they love. You need to do what you love and love what you do in life. We can't refund wasted or lost time. We need to make sure we pay attention to our lives and make sure our dream job doesn't become a dreaded job.

Trying new things in life can be quite daunting. People are often consumed by their personal bubble of preference and are halted by fear of the unknown. Our lives today, where we work, who we know, what we eat, how we dress, just about everything in our lives was new to us at some point. You didn't always like wearing those clothes because you had never worn them before. You didn't always like your spouse or your partner because, at some point in your life, you never knew them. We were all born with no preferences in life. We didn't want coffee in the morning and go to work when we were only 2 weeks old, did we? When you are more open to new experiences, you discover more about yourself.

Often, we are given opportunities to try new things, to do new things and to venture out into the world around us. Unfortunately, we are held back by either the uncertainty or the general "can't be bothered" mentality. The unknown can bring both good and bad things, so focus on how a new experience could benefit you. If everyone had an "I just can't be bothered" attitude, nothing would ever get done in this world.

Obstacles will often bring us to a halt in our lives because we don't know what to do when we face them. When we face a problem we can't handle, or we simply crack under pressure, it can often mean our lives come to a standstill. This is exactly why having passion is so vital to achieving your goals.

The bigger your passion, the bigger your challenges will be. It may seem scary, but with large obstacles comes large rewards. For some, passion is all they have left. Despite being forced into bankruptcy, losing their homes, their families, and their friends, their passion motivates them to get back up and keep going in life. There will be times in our lives when we begin to think, "This is it. I've bitten off more than I can chew, and it's all over now. There is nothing more I can do, and this has just thrown all my hard work in the trash." Although you may think this, you still have hope. You were given your passion for a reason. The best results are achieved when people go through the hard yards and put in the effort. But it can be hard to persist through a challenge or find the strength to face your obstacles and tough times.

Where can you find persistence when facing the tests of life? We may feel as though the whole world is against us, and there's no way out. Sometimes life gets in the way and blocks our view of hope. Occasionally, we need to take a break from everything and have some time to ourselves. When pursuing your goal, don't be afraid to look to the people around you for inspiration. Your family, your friends, God, and even your pets can give you the encouragement you need when you feel down in the dumps. You can find persistence in the most unlikely of places. It could be an old friend that suddenly wanted to reconnect, or a random person handing out flyers on the sidewalk. We don't even need to speak to people to find strength. Seeing someone or looking at motivational image can really inspire you. But no matter what you may face, there is always a way to get through it.

Difference makers and world changers both have one aspect

at their core: they see the bigger picture in life but are still aware of the smaller details. They not only see the individual strokes, but they see the overall grand painting of life. They not only hear each individual note, but they listen to the whole song of the universe. We all need to play our parts in the bigger picture for the better of humanity. We have the power to affect momentous change in the world. Those who have done so have recognised this power inside of them. They have used their passion, power, courage, faith, and wisdom to make a long-lasting impact on the world around them, be it the entire world or simply their own.

A few words can change a person's life forever. When someone asks their partner to marry them, the two little words of "I do" change both people's lives and that of those around them. It's not only words that can make a difference. Actions can speak louder than words in many cases. Even a hug can turn someone's world from complete darkness into hope for a better tomorrow. The things we say and do today ultimately make tomorrow a better, brighter place.

Expect change to come your way and wake up each morning looking for a way to take hold of your day. Right now is the oldest we have ever been and the youngest we will ever be again, so why not make the most out of every day? Wake up with a "bring it on" kind of attitude, rather than "here we go again".

Everyone has one of those days. And you know exactly what I mean by "one of those days". Sometimes it can be hard to be positive all the time because we find ourselves in moments where the birds aren't singing, the sun isn't shining, and you rock up to work soaking wet after a sudden thunderstorm. Here's the thing with life: we need to stop waiting for the storm to pass and start learning how to dance in the rain.

There's always a positive side to every opportunity and challenge that is thrown at us in life. A cut means that your skin will heal and be stronger than it was before. A breakup means you're one heartbreak closer to your true soul mate. If you are fired from your job, it means that a new, better one is coming your way. Even if you can't stay positive all the time, don't let yourself stay down in the dumps. Get back up and tell life to try harder.

History has provided us with countless examples of people who have found their true passion and used it to make their mark in the world. It may not be apparent at first, but you may very well be a world changer, a mountain mover, and a leader of a new generation. Take Leonardo Da Vinci, for instance. We all know his name, yet he lived over 500 years ago. He found just about all of his passions, from inventing to painting, music to architecture and everything in between. Over the many years since then, he is recognised as one of the greatest figures in human history. Da Vinci saw ways in which the world could be improved and focused his passions on achieving a better future. Be it creating the first helicopter model, or painting "The Last Supper", or capturing the unique smile of the Mona Lisa, he worked tirelessly and found joy in every area of his life. One could claim that his main passion was life itself. He learnt how to master so many skills over his life, but unfortunately, immortality was not one of them. History has given us countless examples of people who have found their passion and used it to change the world, either intentionally or not. So, 500 years from now, will you be remembered for your passion?

You may have a rough idea what your passion is, however,

you're not entirely sure. Nothing's stopping you now. Have a crack at something new. It could only do you a world of good. But not yet, you're just a few moments away from finishing this chapter.

On that note, what have you learnt in this book? You and I have been through a lot in the past 19 chapters. But now, our journey is drawing to a close. Between all the lessons about changing your life and making a mark in the world, you've heard stories of successes, skills, and good times over my own life and that of others. We've been on the clock once or twice, we've ventured into the jungle and had some wild experiences with greedy monkeys, birds of a feather and unfortunately the people you are stuck with in life. We've visited the mask shop and bought a few leashes for our lips. We've weighed our world, seen society's greatest flaw, been to the courtroom and travelled all through time, not to mention all the other places we've been.

Finding meaning is never easy in life. It's something we all have but never fully understand what it is until it has already passed us by. After the somewhat 210 pages you've read, after all the lessons, you should have a rough idea of what your meaning is or how you can find it at least. Many go through life never knowing their true calling. If they find it, they second-guess themselves or consider whether it's theirs or someone else's. That's exactly why God is the best person to turn to. Praying about it might just get you the answer you are looking for. I urge you to utilise your lessons to find your true calling and meaning. You may have a handful, possibly 15 or 20, or even more. But even if you have only one, then I am glad to have shared this journey with you, learning along the way as we ventured into every new chapter and page.

Now clean the slate of all negativity, adopt a fresh new

perspective and tackle life head-on. It's not going to be a sudden "BAM! Oh look, I found my meaning. Yay". No, it's going to be a lot harder than that, and it's going to take you a few tries before you find "the one". But that's why we are given such a long time on earth. Look at it this way, the average human being has a life expectancy of 71 years. That's a total of 25,915 days (not including leap years) which is 621,960 hours which is a lot of minutes and even more seconds in an average life. But here's the thing: you aren't the average human being. You are a unique model with the skills and talents of no other person on this earth.

With a little patience, you can find your passion-driven meaning in life by applying the lessons you have learnt in this book. Before long, you will see everything change around you as you understand and apply these new lessons. I really hope that you've got a lot out of this, as I have.

But what's next?

Now you have some of my knowledge, the ball is in your court. Don't only change your life but change the lives of those around you. Go out and be a world changer, a mountain mover, a sea crosser, a dream liver. Be the hero of your own story and the person God wants you to be. Make the best of every year, month, day, hour, minute, and every second you have, as you adventure through life, making memories, good decisions, bad decisions and hopefully having a bit of fun along the way. After all, you did take it from a teenager.

ABOUT THE AUTHOR

Scott Bradbrook can usually be found working on university assignments, tutoring high school students or sharpening his salsa skills. But between all of that, he is an aspiring author and editor. Writing his first book, *Take It From A Teenager*, at the age of 15, he went on to publish it just shy of his 19th birthday and second year at university. Majoring in Creative Writing and Mathematical Sciences in his Bachelor of Arts (Advanced), Scott focusses on bettering himself and the world around him every day. Having trained in martial arts for over 10 years and excelling in his schooling, achieving the Long Tan Award and receiving the Mary Fountain Shield at Christian Brothers College, he has spent much of his life gaining knowledge and wisdom from renowned public speakers such as Tony Robbins, Brendan Burchard and Joel Osteen. Between playing with his dog, watching movies with friends and spending time with family, Scott is continuously writing and generating new ideas for future books and series.

For more information on his upcoming books, visit www.scottbradbrook.com or follow Scott on his social media:

Facebook.com/sb.scottbradbrook

Instagram.com/Scott_Bradbrook

Twitter.com/ScottBradbrook

www.ingramcontent.com/pod-product-compliance
Lightning Source LLC
LaVergne TN
LVHW041153080426
835511LV00006B/577